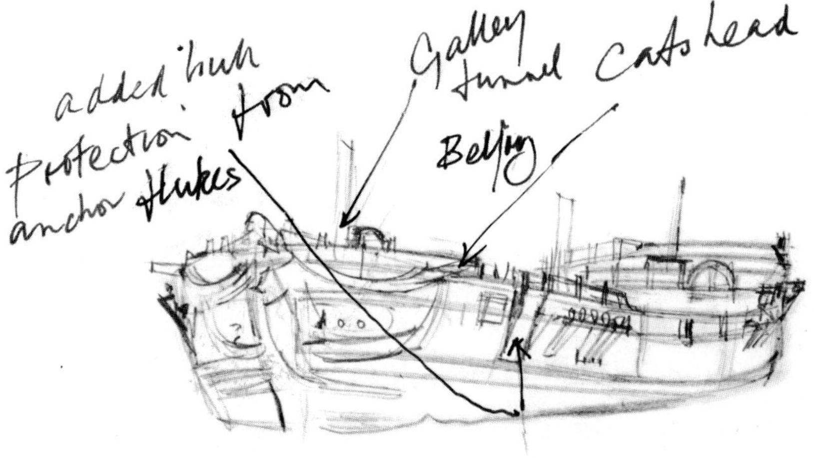

THE MARINE PAINTINGS OF CHRIS MAYGER

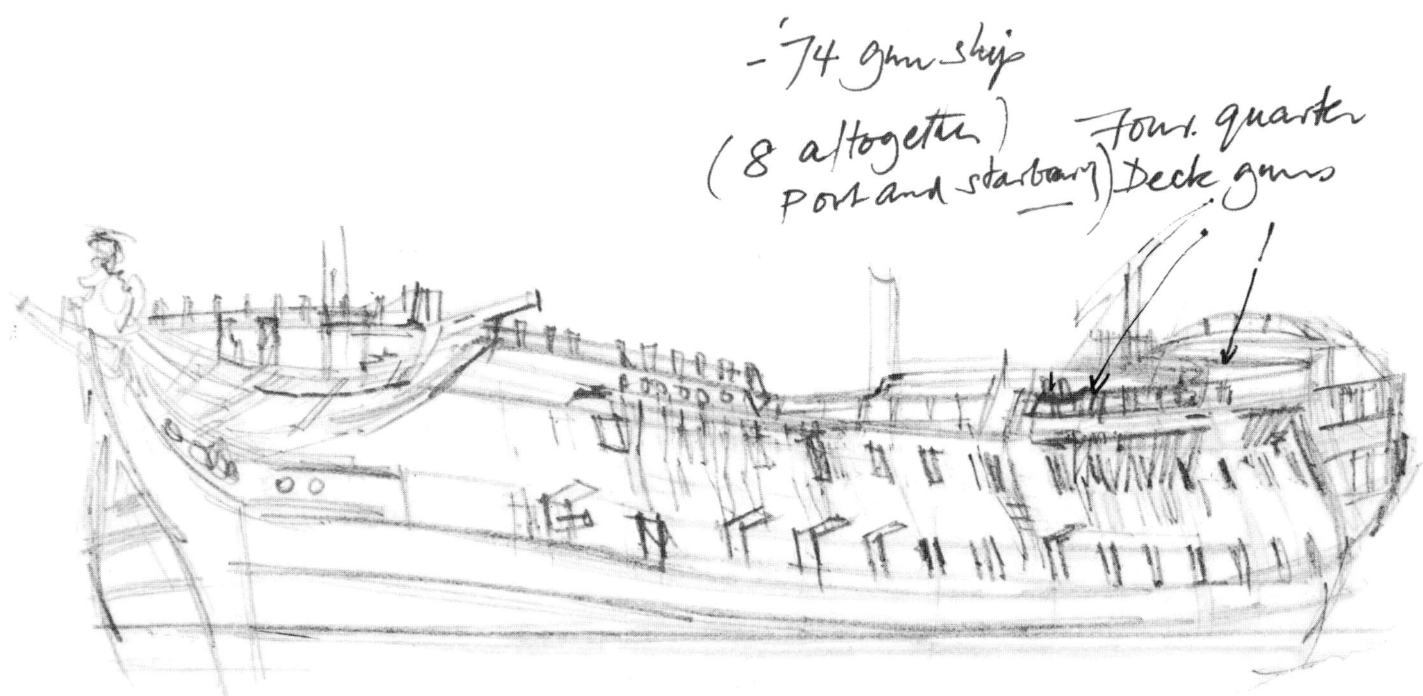

The Marine Paintings of
Chris Mayger

Edited and Introduced by David Larkin

Pan Books Ltd.
London and Sydney

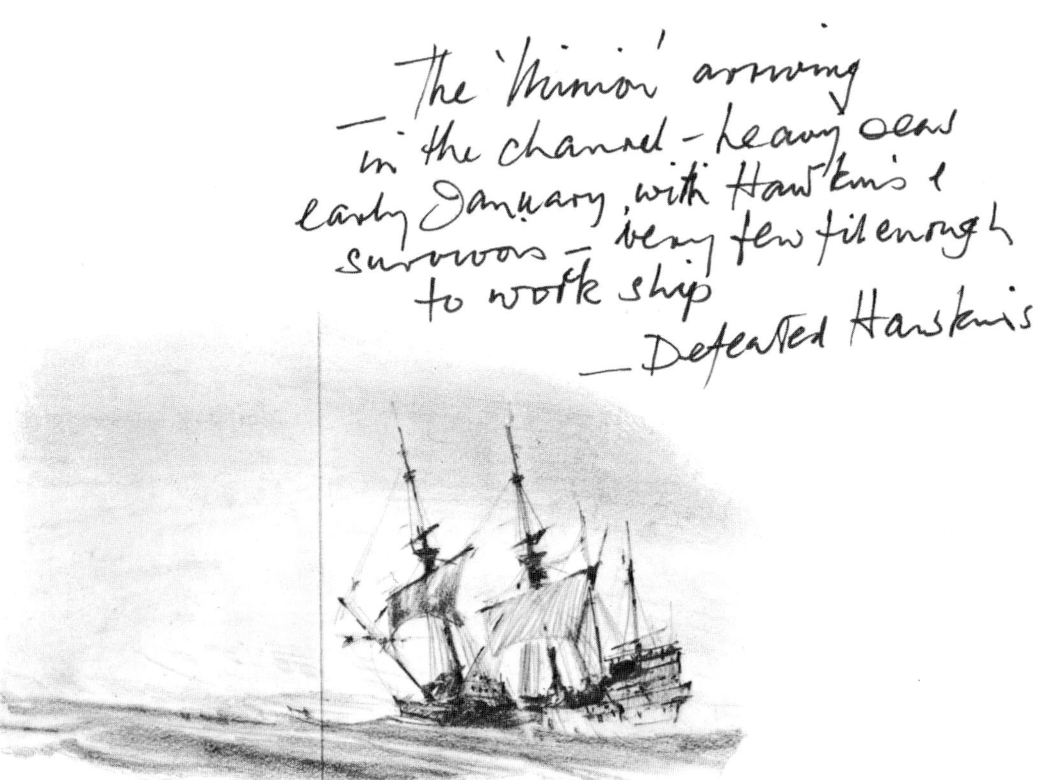

Our thanks to the publishers who cooperated with us on material
previously reproduced as book cover illustrations.

We are also grateful to the private owners of the artists' work.

An original PEACOCK PRESS/BANTAM BOOK

THE MARINE PAINTINGS OF CHRIS MAYGER

This edition published 1976 by Pan Books Ltd.
Cavaye Place, London SW10 9PG
ISBN 0 330 24832 4

Published simultaneously in the United States and Canada

PRINTED IN THE UNITED STATES OF AMERICA
By Regensteiner Press, Chicago

Six years ago in the Bay of Biscay a cruise ship was going through a force nine gale. There was one man on deck — a passenger. He braced himself against a stanchion so that both hands were free to operate his home movie camera and began filming what the sea was doing. If it came out he knew it would be useful. Later, at home with a little editing machine, he could stop the print and look closely at the stopped motion of the waves and spray, and make sketches.

Chris Mayger was in the process of changing his career. His intention was to try to paint the sea and the ships that moved with it.

He was born in Deptford, South London, and as a boy would go to Greenwich Pier, in the heart of the Port of London, and sketch the working tugs and steamers that plied the English coast. He decided on a career in commercial art. After his studies at Camberwell School of Art he joined an art studio that specialized in industrial subjects. When the war clouds were gathering in 1938 he thought of joining the Navy, but was talked out of it by friends. Then came the war and Chris volunteered for the Army. From there he tried to transfer to the Navy but, because he was a non-commissioned officer, was refused. After the war he returned to his old business, gradually developing all the skills that a commercial artist needs. By this time he had become interested in drawing aircraft and ships, and could draw them quickly and accurately. A friend noticed this and advised him to join an advertising agency as a visualizer (this is someone who can render ideas into slick and believable sketches). Despite the routine of running the day-to-day work of the agency studio, Chris found time to pursue his growing love of marine subjects by working for some freelance clients. Combined with the pressures of the office, this meant a busy life, and the long hours spent commuting were especially exhausting for someone who draws and needs peace

heavy squally sky
broken lighter sky
beyond flagship
— heavy rain

the Defeat of John Hawkins
the storm swept Fleet — west of Madeira (Pages 40-44)
— Jesus in the lead towing her longboat
likewise the following ships Minion, Swallow etc.

— sea - long swell
general colour storm greys
& grey greens.

— ship under reefed foresail +
lanteen sail on mizzen.

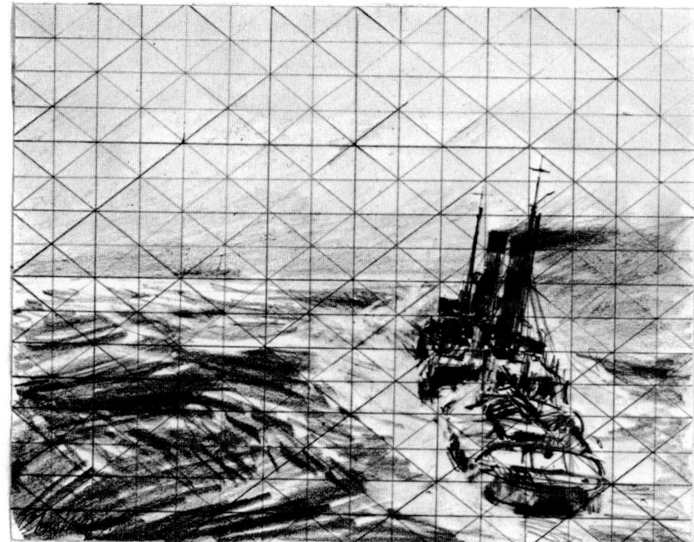

Rescue Tug — Foundation Franklin if
(—she rolled as if she really enjoyed it)
Page 15.

and quiet in order to concentrate.

A change of working circumstances led Chris to decide on a full time life of self-employment. For a working commercial artist the change to a freelance career is often a big step, and Chris Mayger, being so long a studio man, was full of doubts. Gradually, though, with strong support from his wife and the help of old contacts, work began to come to him. And eventually the first paperback cover.

At this time paperback covers for the masses had lost most of the overacted drawing, blood, sex and kitsch quotients that had once been thought necessary to

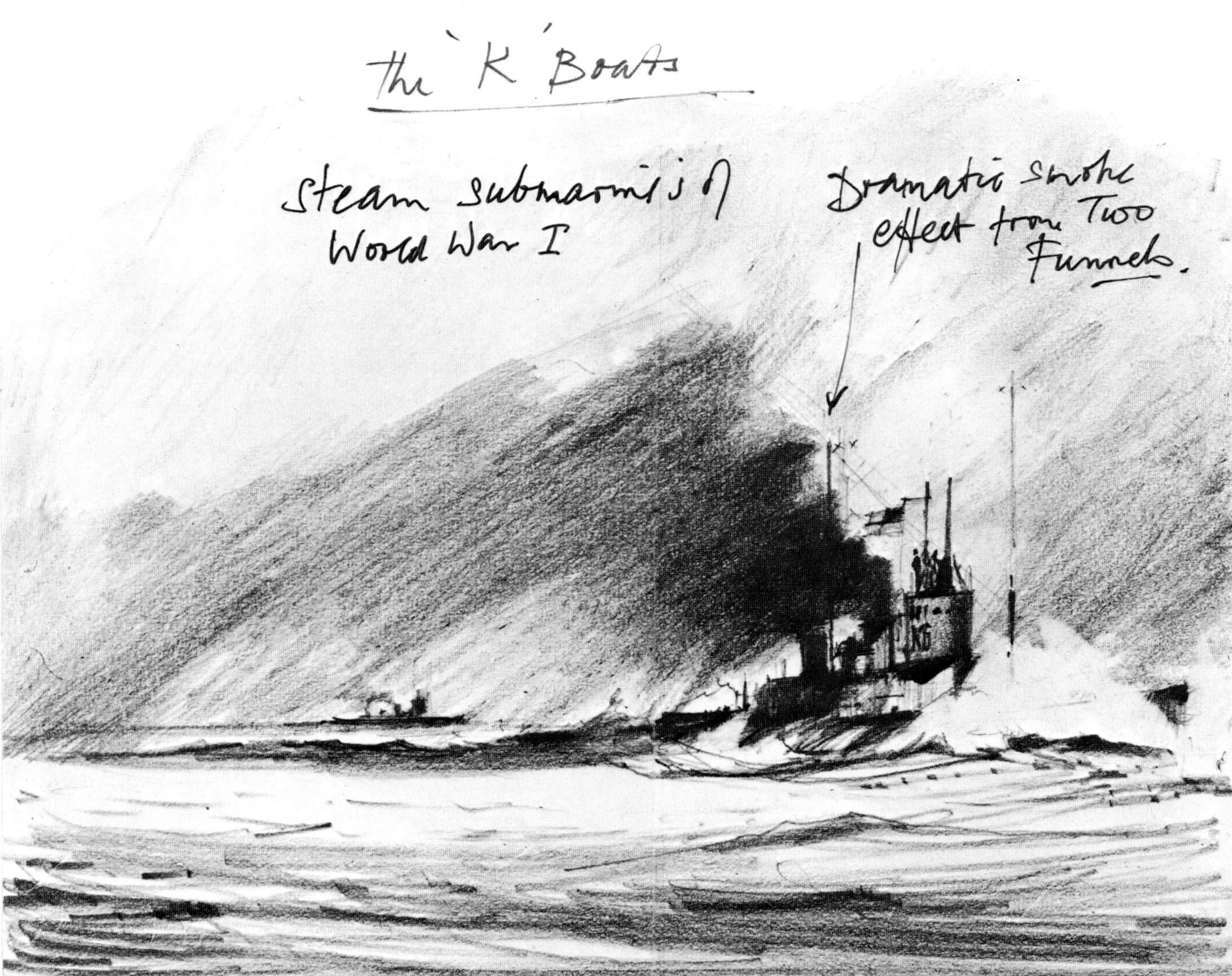

attract a pulp audience. Readers were more discerning and standards were rising in printing, binding and presentation. Paperback art directors were now looking for specialist illustrators. Chris was a natural.

For his first covers he prepared several pencil roughs, thinking that this was what publishers required. In fact, in presenting his ideas this way he was continuing the advertising agency practice. Now this is fine for the publisher's art director, but sometimes, in order to satisfy colleagues, he can be tempted to use the best elements from all the sketches and that usually results in a bad cover.

On these commissions Chris had to consider very important requirements. The publisher will always need room for the title, author and blurb, yet the illustrator must execute a cohesive and satisfying painting. Also, it is common nowadays for cover illustrations to embrace the entire wrapper, so that the important incident is on the right-hand side of the picture. The wrap-around illustration actually does very little for the display of the edition when it is in position on the booksellers' shelves, but it does wonders for the salesmen who promote the book to the stores by showing the covers in flat form before they have been bound

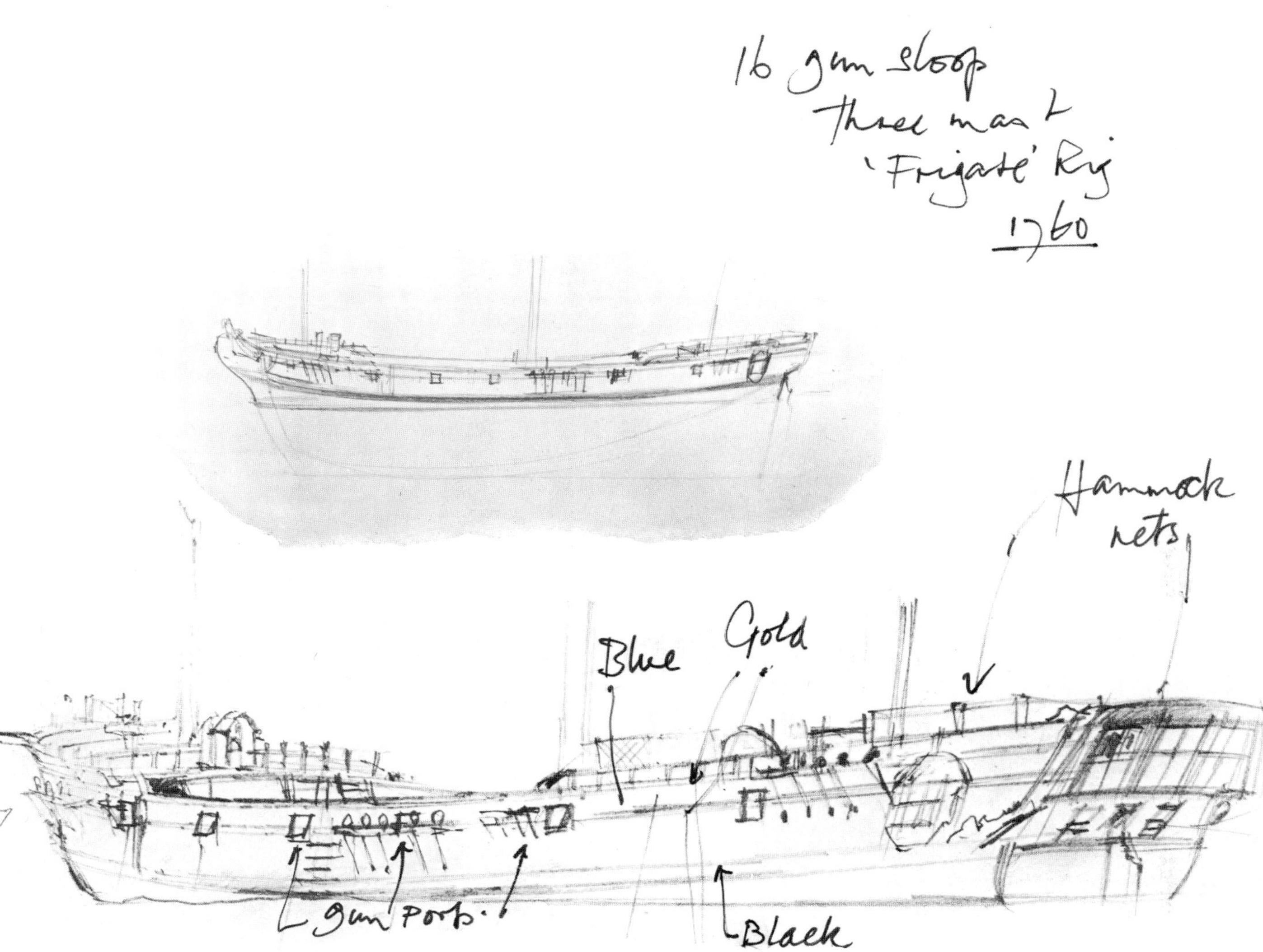

onto the books. This graphic approach also enhances the 'epic' features of some books and is a bonus for the lovers of good illustration.

The Fleet Without a Friend (Plate 2) seemed to be fine when finished except that the smoke, billowing hugely from right to left, was a problem. The publishers needed even more smoke to act as a platform for all the titling. So back the painting went to the artist, and the ship burned still more fiercely.

At this time, apart from referring to his home movie, Chris was laboring in other ways at getting his seas to move. He looked at the paintings of Frank Mason, Norman Wilkinson and Montague Dawson, searching for the painterly approach. He needn't have worried: one of his first paperback cover illustrations went on exhibition at the Royal Society of Marine Artists. His style was developing anyway, employing gouache in a method created from previous disciplines. Happy accidents with the brush and the knowledge of when to leave well enough alone when something interesting occurred contributed to his growing confidence.

Visits to archives and museums with his sketch pad taught him that photographs of ships and other objects are useful reference,

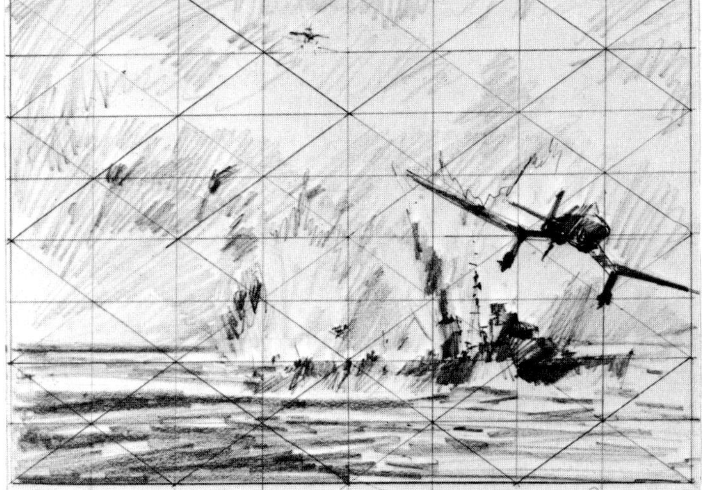

but that the sea can't be copied this way: it must be created in the painting itself. Where Mayger's paintings excel is in the movement of sea, fog and mist around steel and wooden hulls and against rocks and sand.

All his publishers were now benefiting from his experience. What he learned on one cover was employed on the next. Chris studied books on sailing and weather and in particular the Beaufort Scale (the standard maritime table for measuring wind force) to find out what happens when wind speed affects the sea in conditions described in the text. All his paintings get their atmosphere from the mood of the sky, and this depends on the weather and time of day. When starting the painting Chris scales up his sketch and draws carefully with pencil. Then he begins to color the sky, sometimes taking three days to get it right.

The painting for *Sink the Tirpitz* (Plate 10) is unique because, as with many famous events, there were no photographs of the action, only aerial views. The small flag belatedly indicates an air raid warning.

With *Leviathan* (Plate 12) invention was the requirement. The ship is fictitious and seemed to have characteristics of both the *Queen Elizabeth* and the *Queen Mary*. We can

Clipper Ship — again atmosphere
heavy threatening sky
laden sea - colour reflected
from sky — sail reduced
or being reduced by crew .

Cold Blue.
to pale Viridian

Pale green
to white

Sky
reflection
on sea

Pale Naples
Yellow through Blue Grey.

Stormy sun light
from R/hand
side

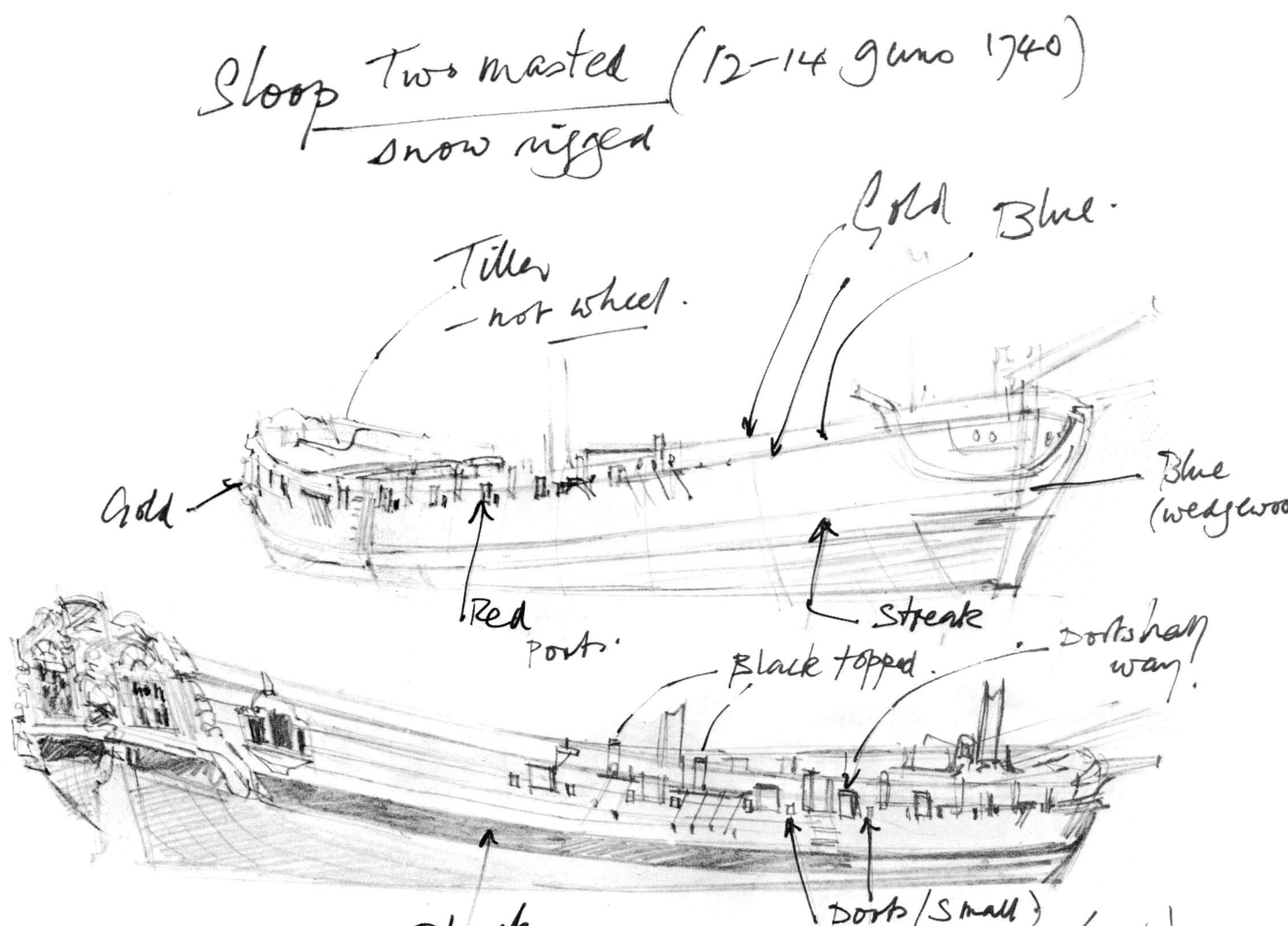

note that the bridge bears a resemblance to the *Queen Mary's*.

The sails on the ship in *Pacific Ordeal* (Plate 13) were to check its rolling while towing the other ships. The dory is standing by because the line kept breaking.

Crete 1941 (Plate 3) was a difficult assignment because, although this was an actual event, there were no pictorial references to the actual terrain and ships involved. Yet when Chris showed the painting to friends who had taken part in this evacuation, they said that that was how it was.

There were many illustrated accounts of the most famous sinking of all. Most drawings show the sinking liner with all its lights on, but in *The Maiden Voyage of the Titanic* (Plate 5) Chris chose the moment when a lot of people didn't yet know she was going down and still believed her to be unsinkable. He originally painted distress rockets going up from the ship, but these detracted from the wording required on the back cover and had to be removed.

When concerned with military and historical subjects the present-day paperback cover, despite its restrictions as a miniature, often presents a more accurate record of true events and disasters than the so-called 'official' art. This was sometimes

executed without quite enough research and
a little too much guesswork. Here, then, is
the work of a man who, with his concern
for accuracy and detail and his sense of
drama and excitement, has brought many
new readers to books.

My feeling as a designer is that Chris
Mayger is just passing through the
paperback industry and is on the way to
serious recognition as a painter with its
greater challenges and rewards.

David Larkin   **January 1976**

1) The Flying Enterprise
1953
Private Collection
Mrs. M. Mayger
*My only oil, I did it from
a news item, for pleasure.*

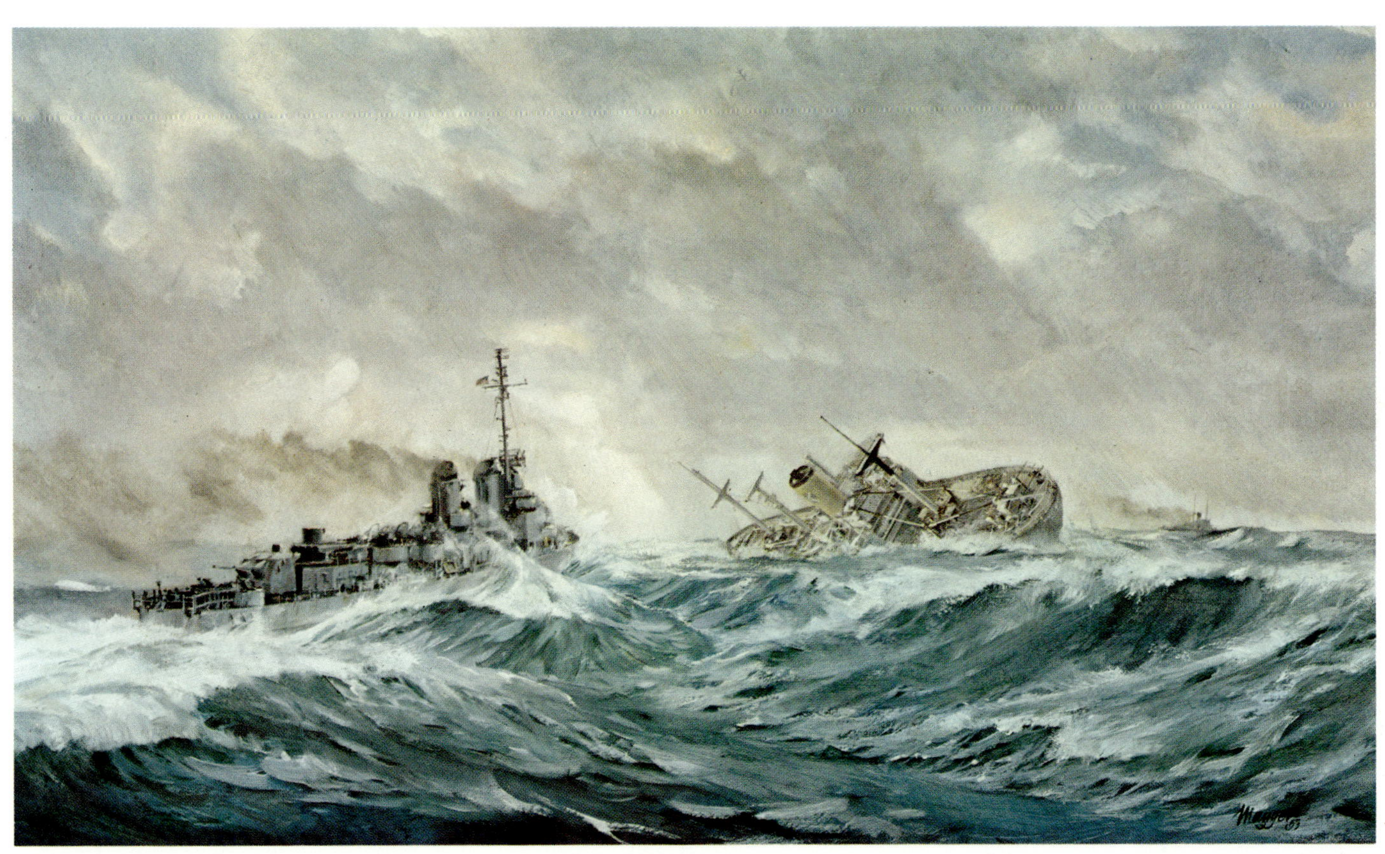

2) The Fleet Without a Friend
by John Vader
May 1971
New English Library

This is the Bretagne *sinking as the French fleet are caught between the Vichy and the Allies.*

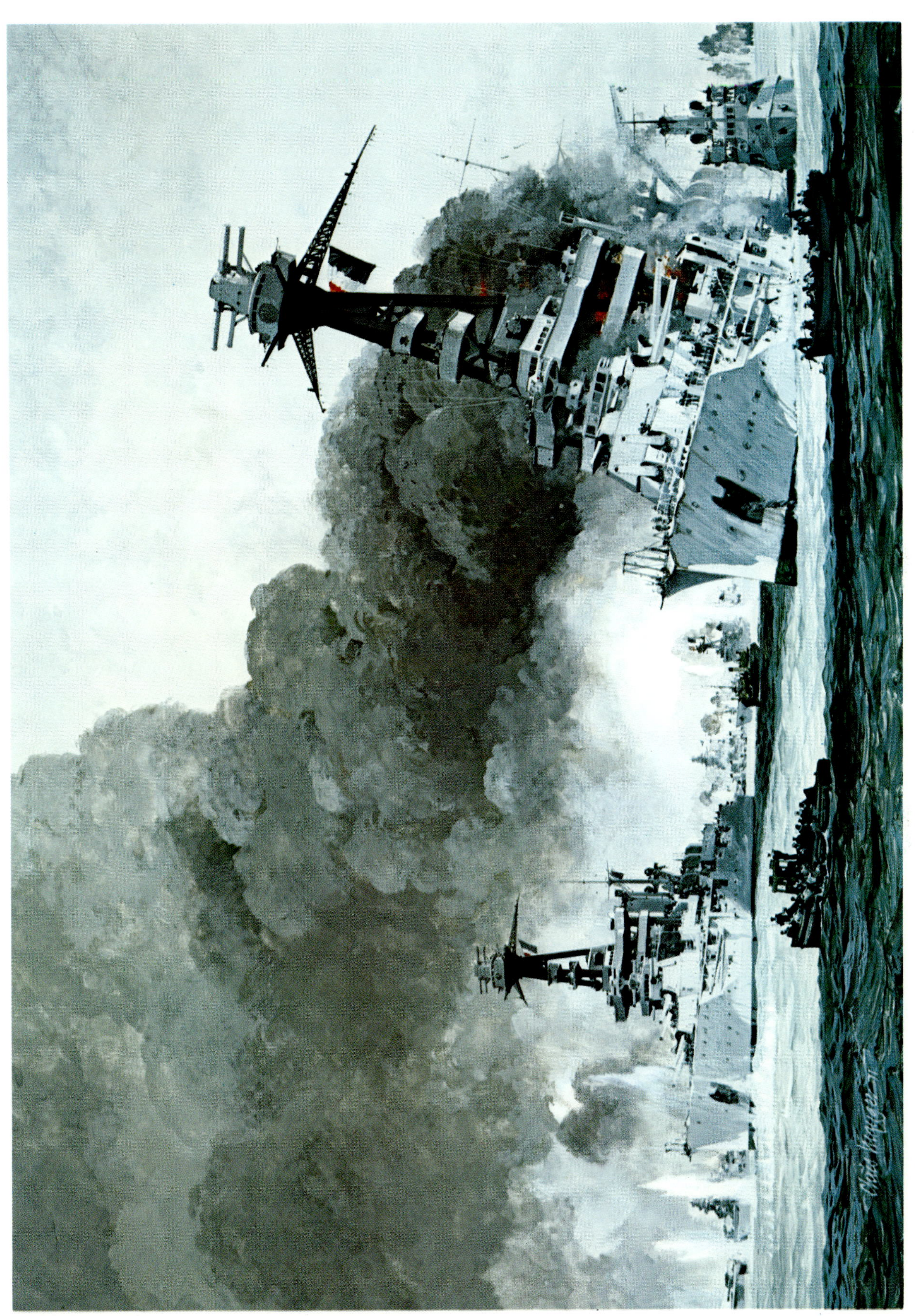

3) Crete 1941 – The Battle at Sea
by David A. Thomas
May 1975
New English Library
I had to devise the destroyers as there was little reference available.

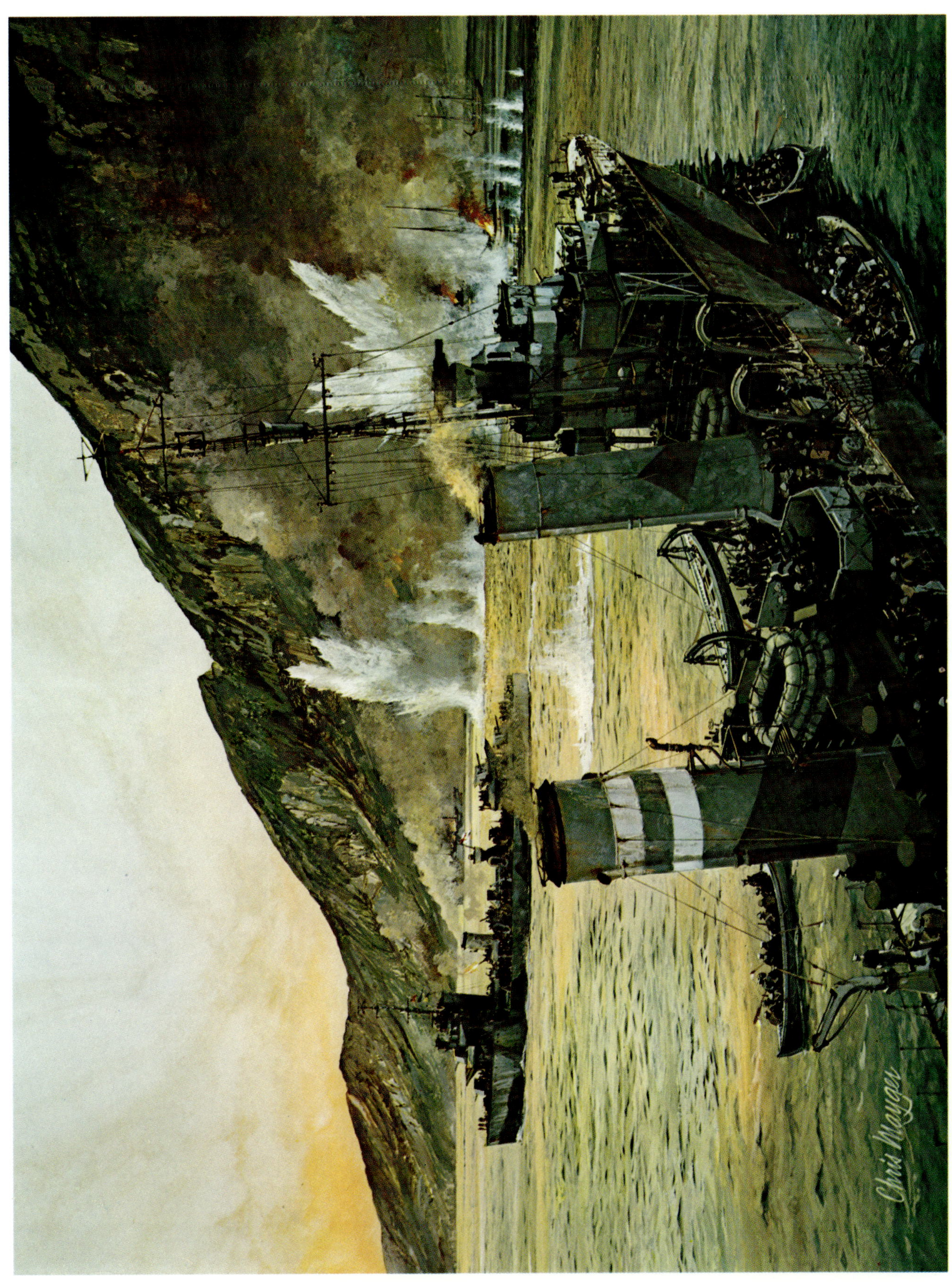

4) Lilliput Fleet
by A. Cecil Hampshire
July 1975
New English Library

The trawlers had only 3″ or 4″ guns to use against aircraft,
so I used the gun platform as the focal point.

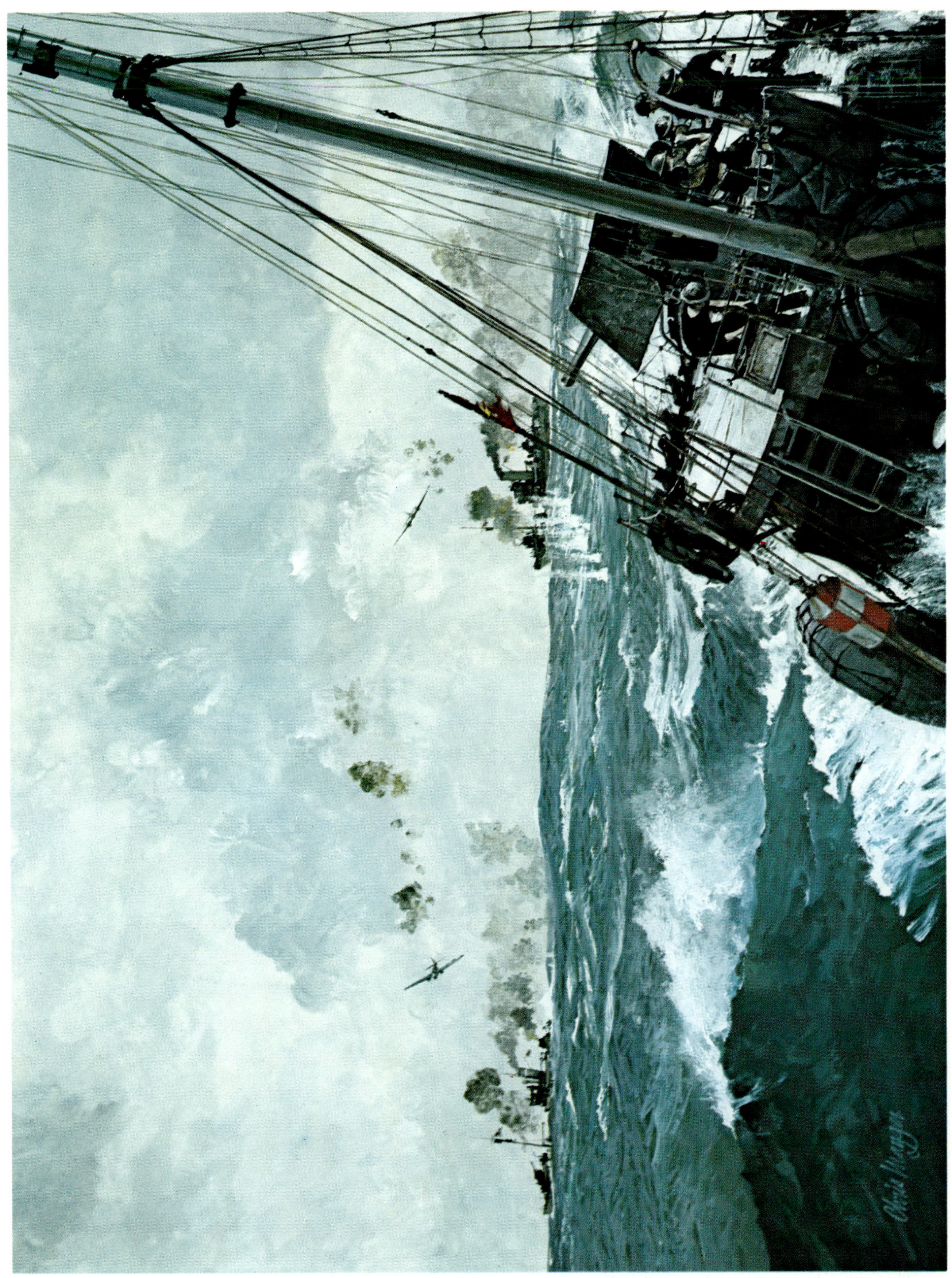

5) The Maiden Voyage of the Titanic
by Geoffrey Marcus
September 1975
New English Library

This is when the last of the lifeboats is being lowered and there are still many people aboard the sinking ship.

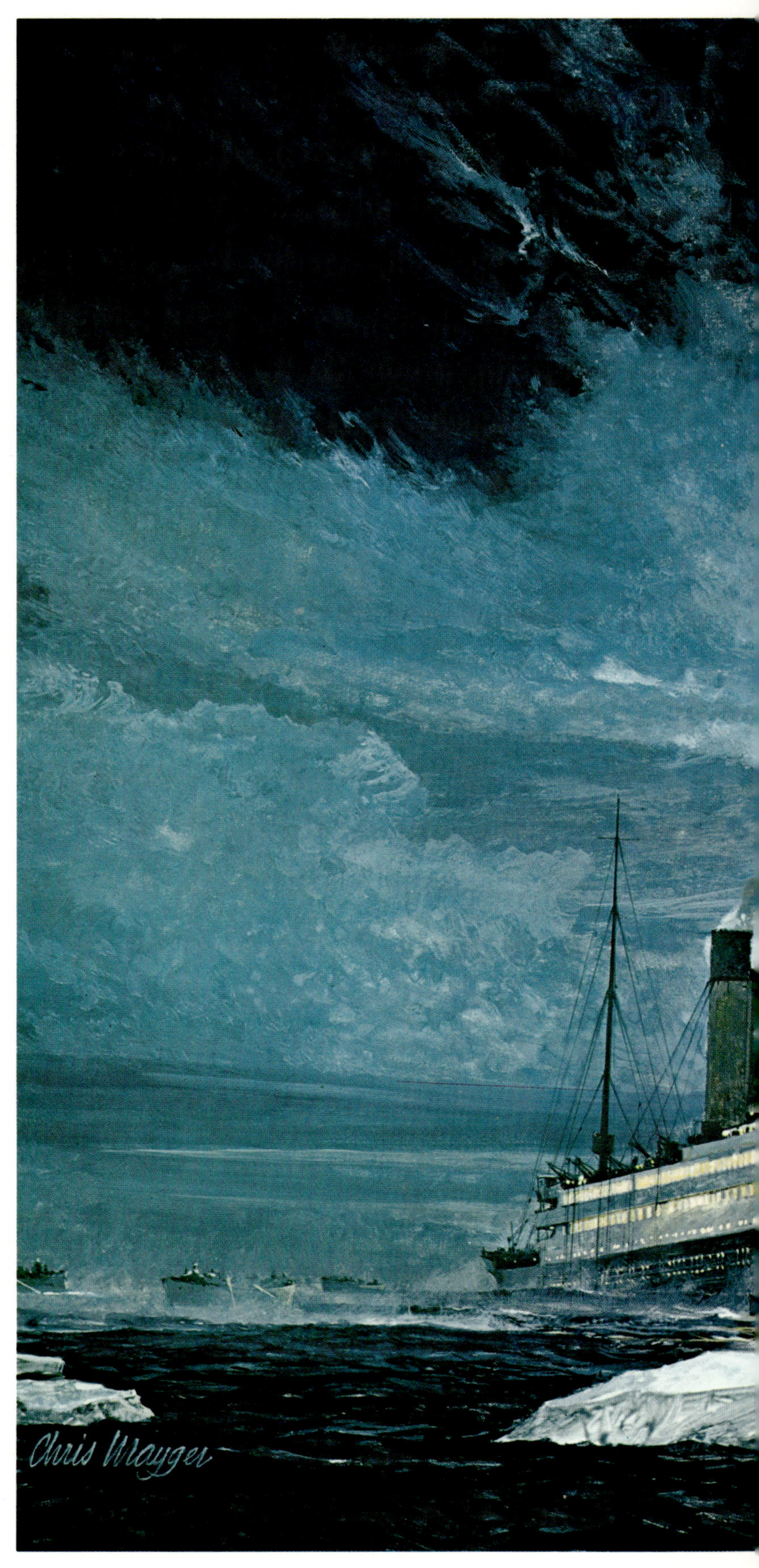

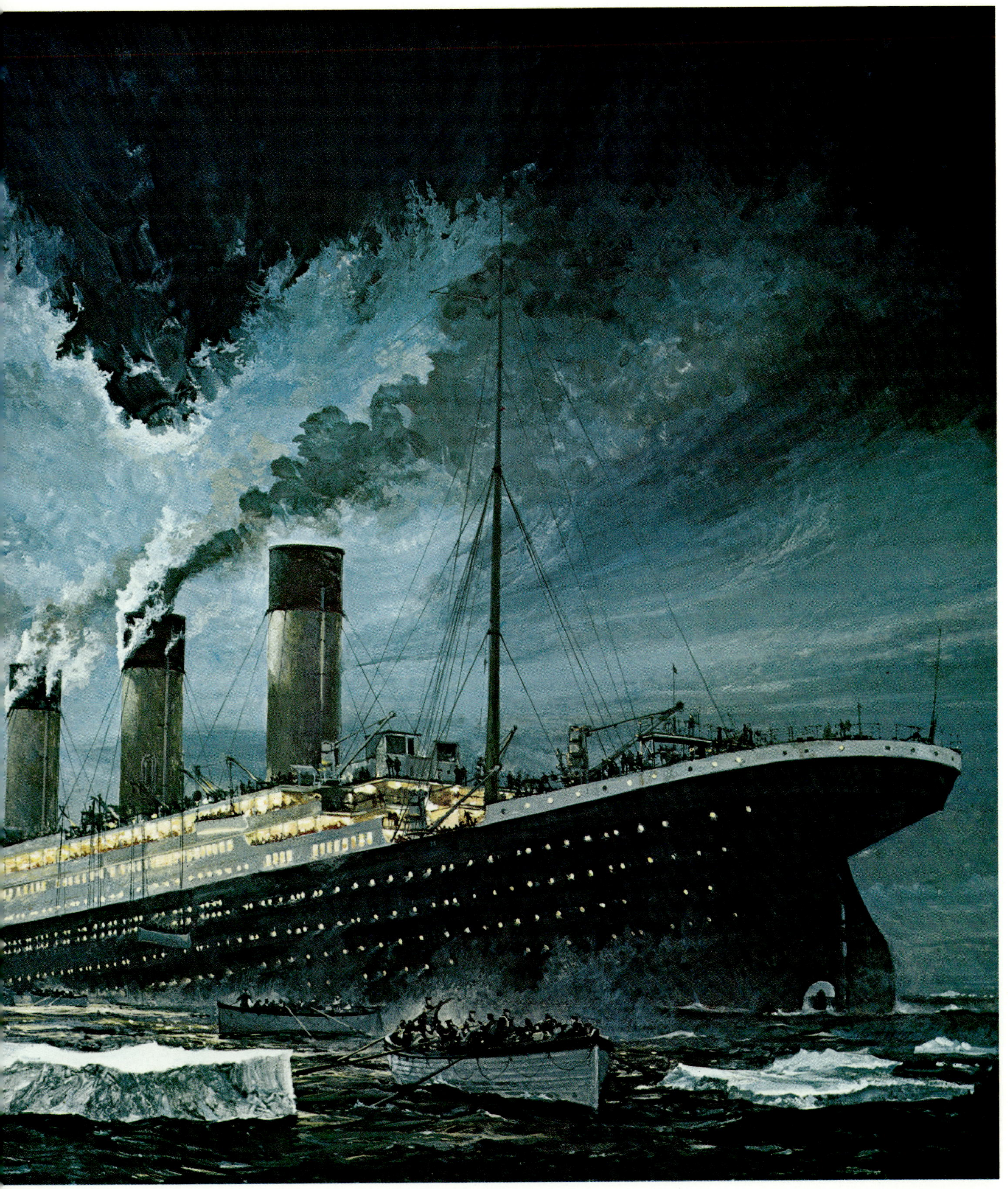

6) Three Corvettes
by Nicholas Monsarrat
May 1972
Mayflower/Granada Publishing
*I would handle it differently now that I have more reference on
Flower Class Corvettes.*

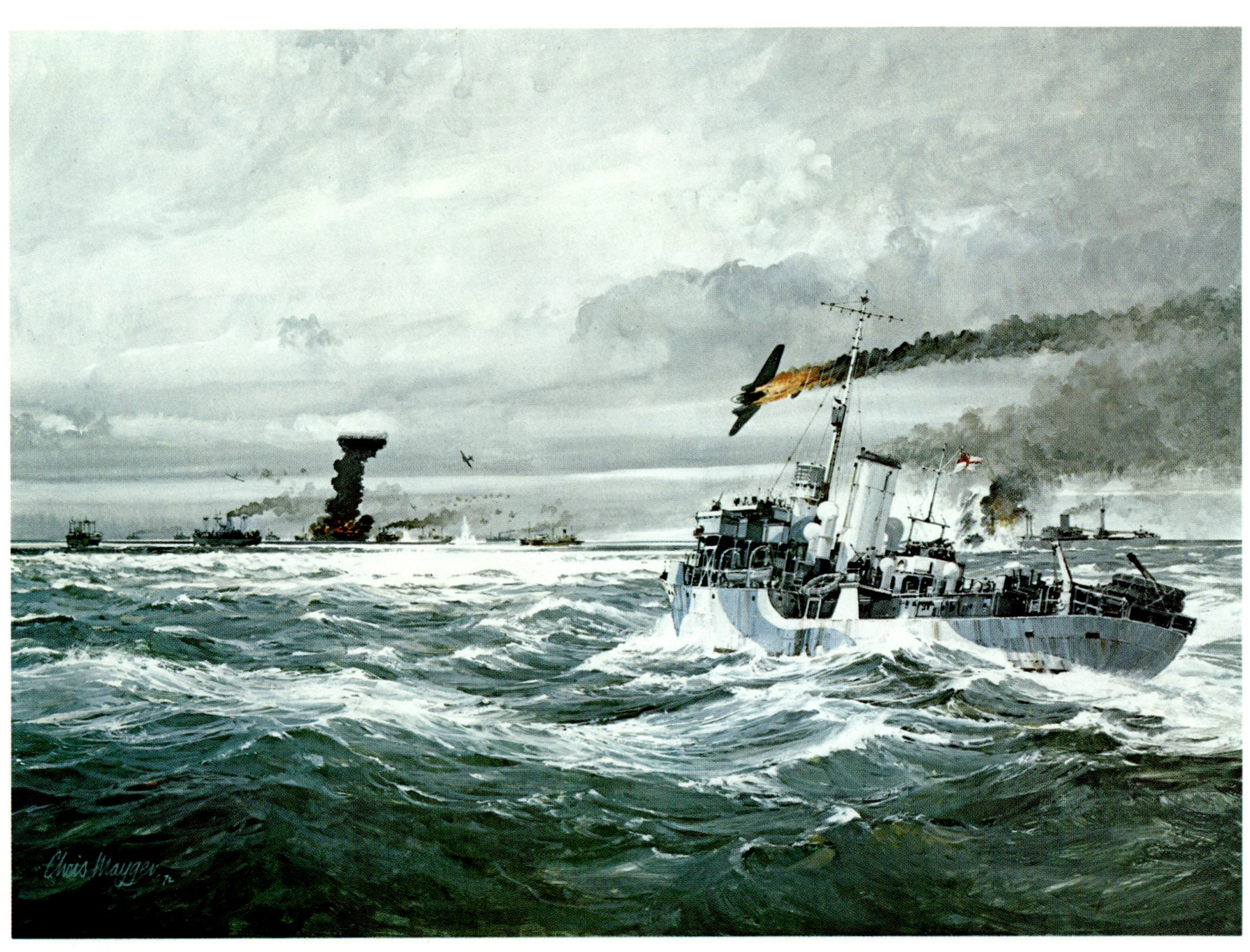

7) *Detail from*
Three Corvettes
by Nicholas Monsarrat
May 1972
Mayflower/Granada Publishing

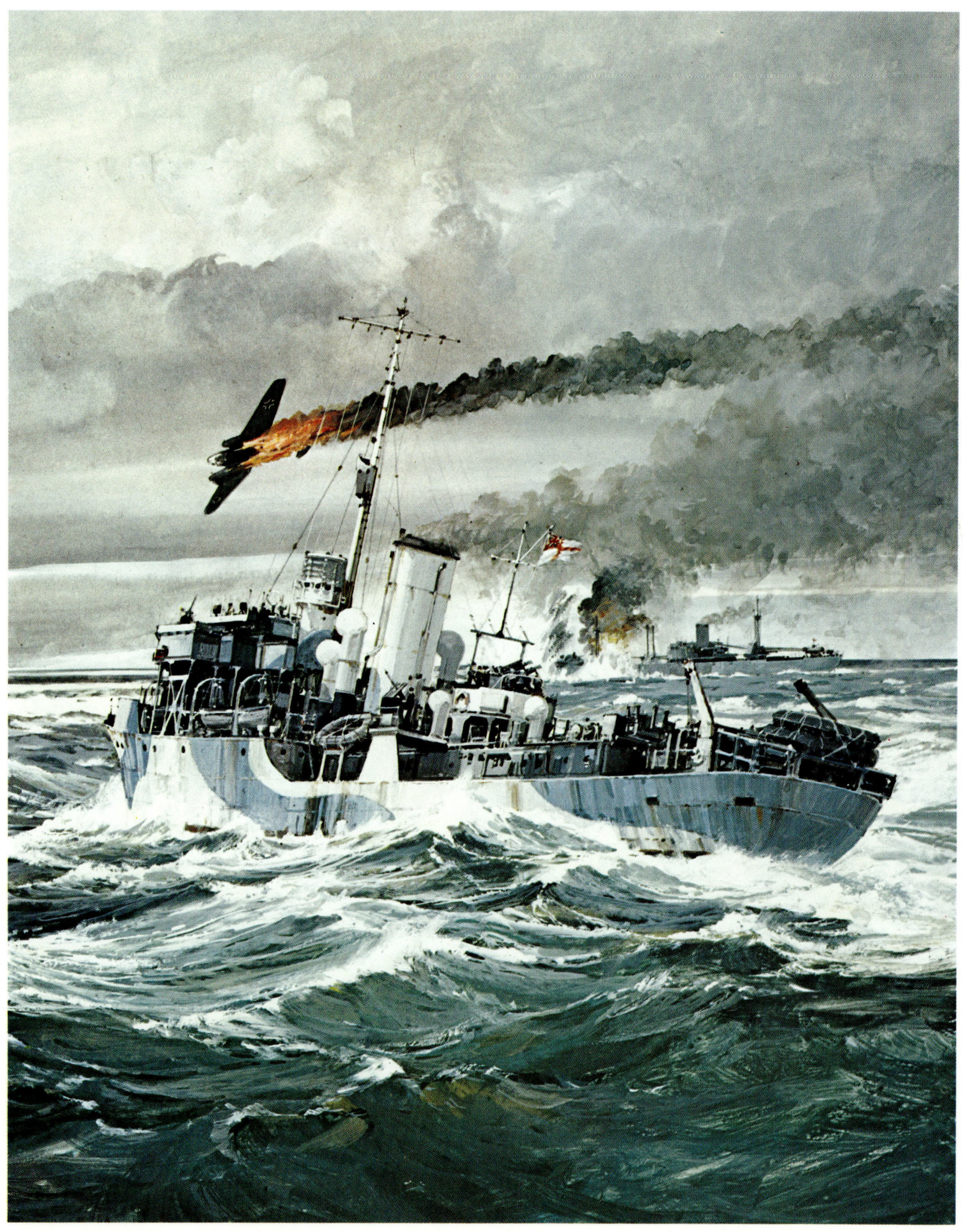

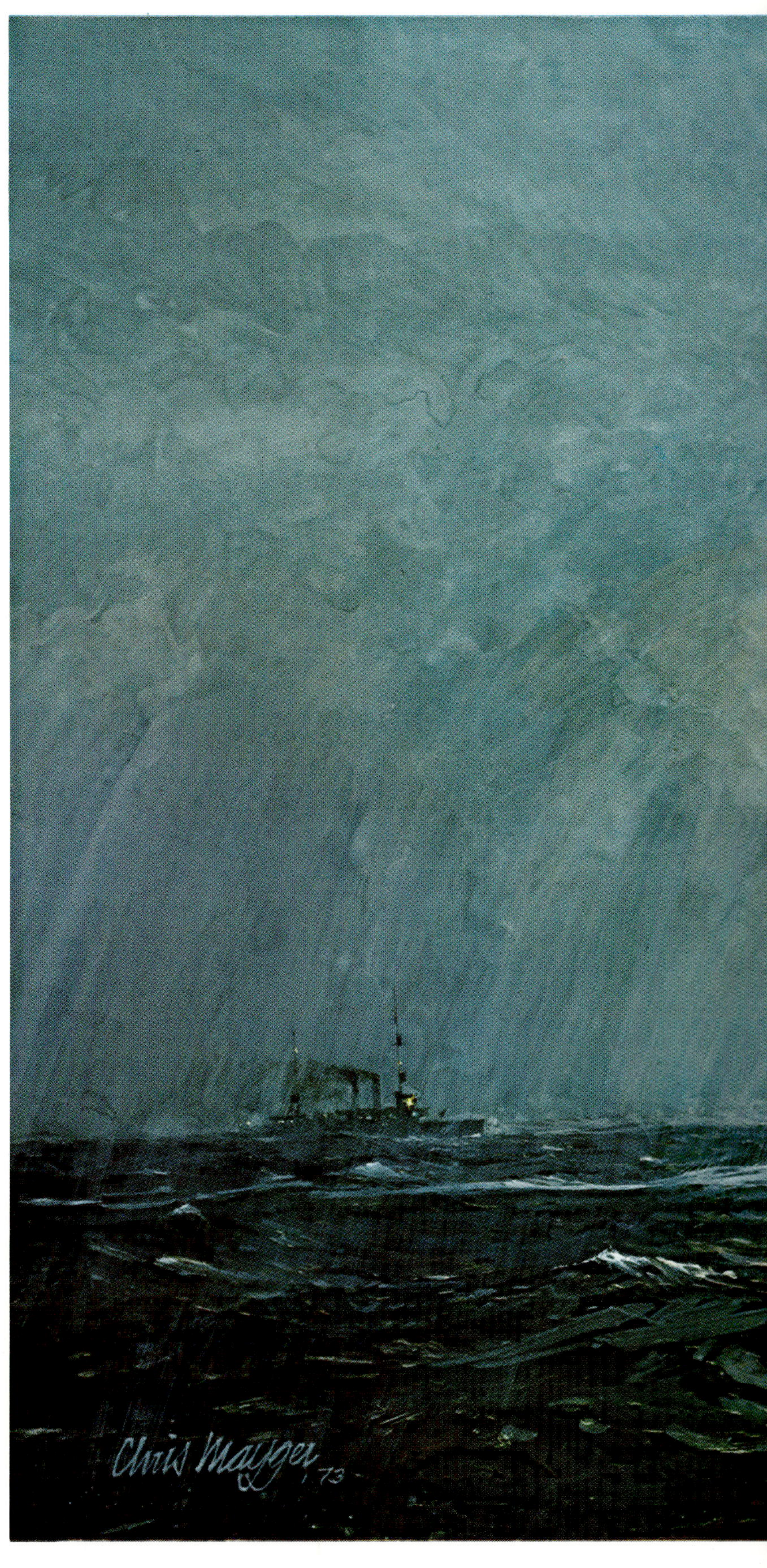

8) The Wake of the Gertrude Lüth
by Patrick O'Hara
February 1973
Panther/Granada Publishing

*I had difficulty imagining the lighting effect of the floodlights
and the orange star shell described by the Author.*

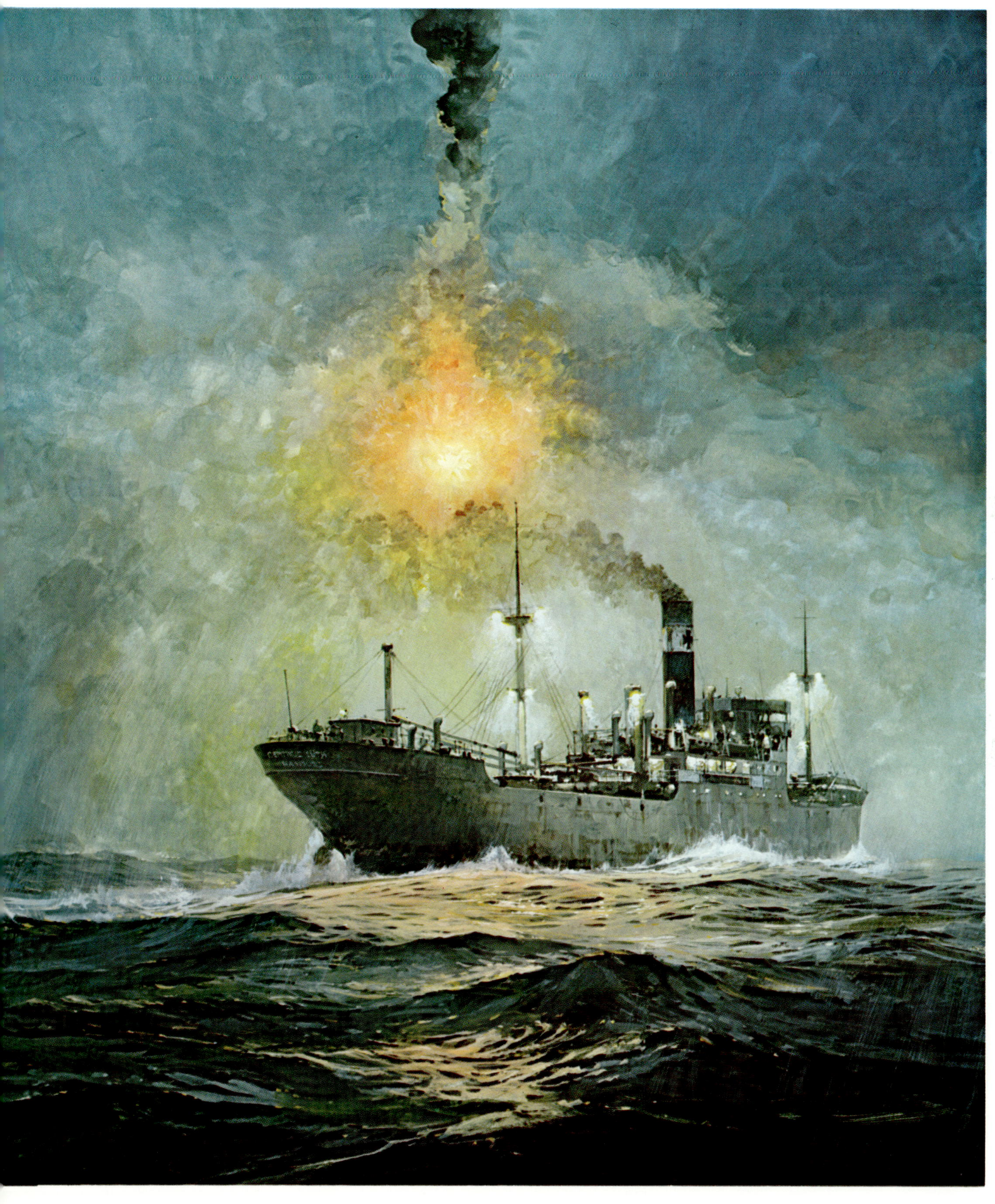

9) Surface!
by Alexander Fullerton
June 1973
Mayflower/Granada Publishing

*I don't really like summer seas – too travelogue-like, I prefer
cold gray, winter seas.*

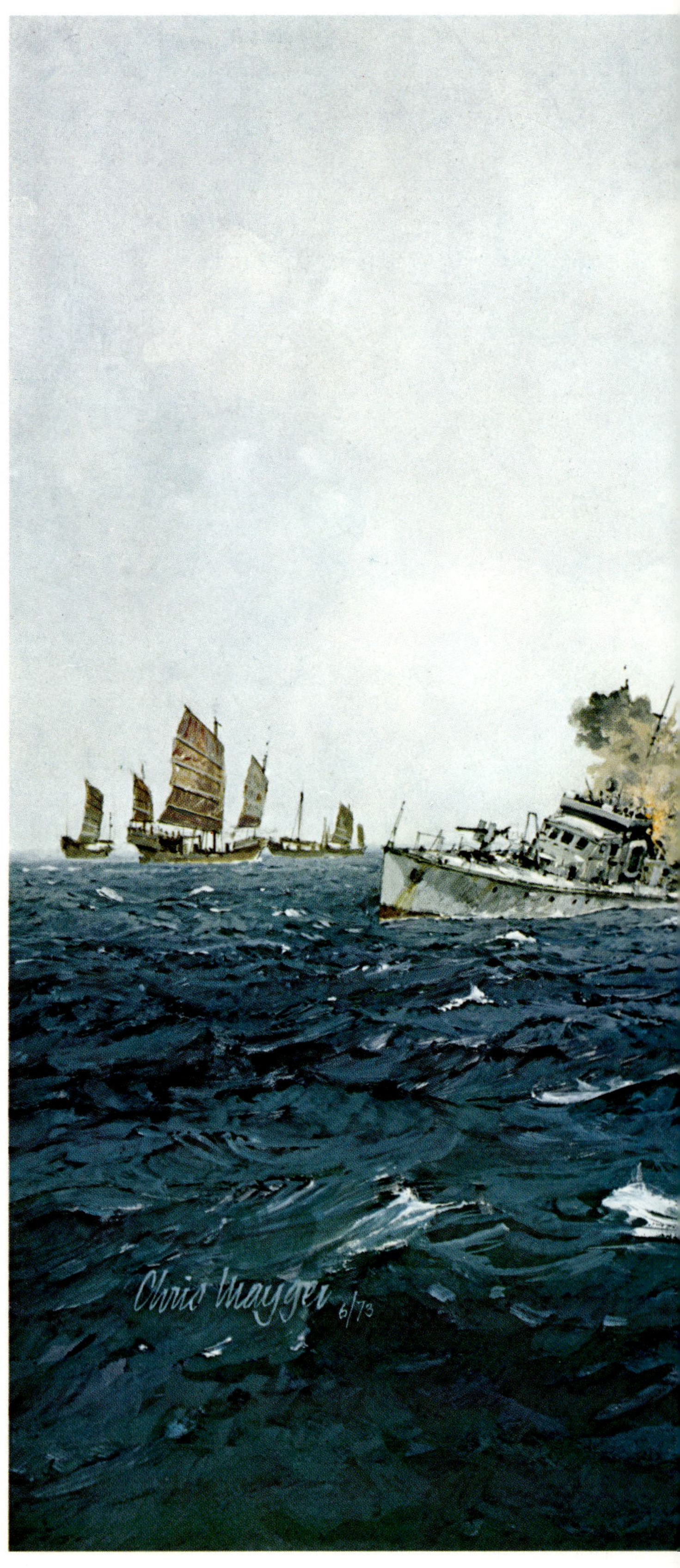

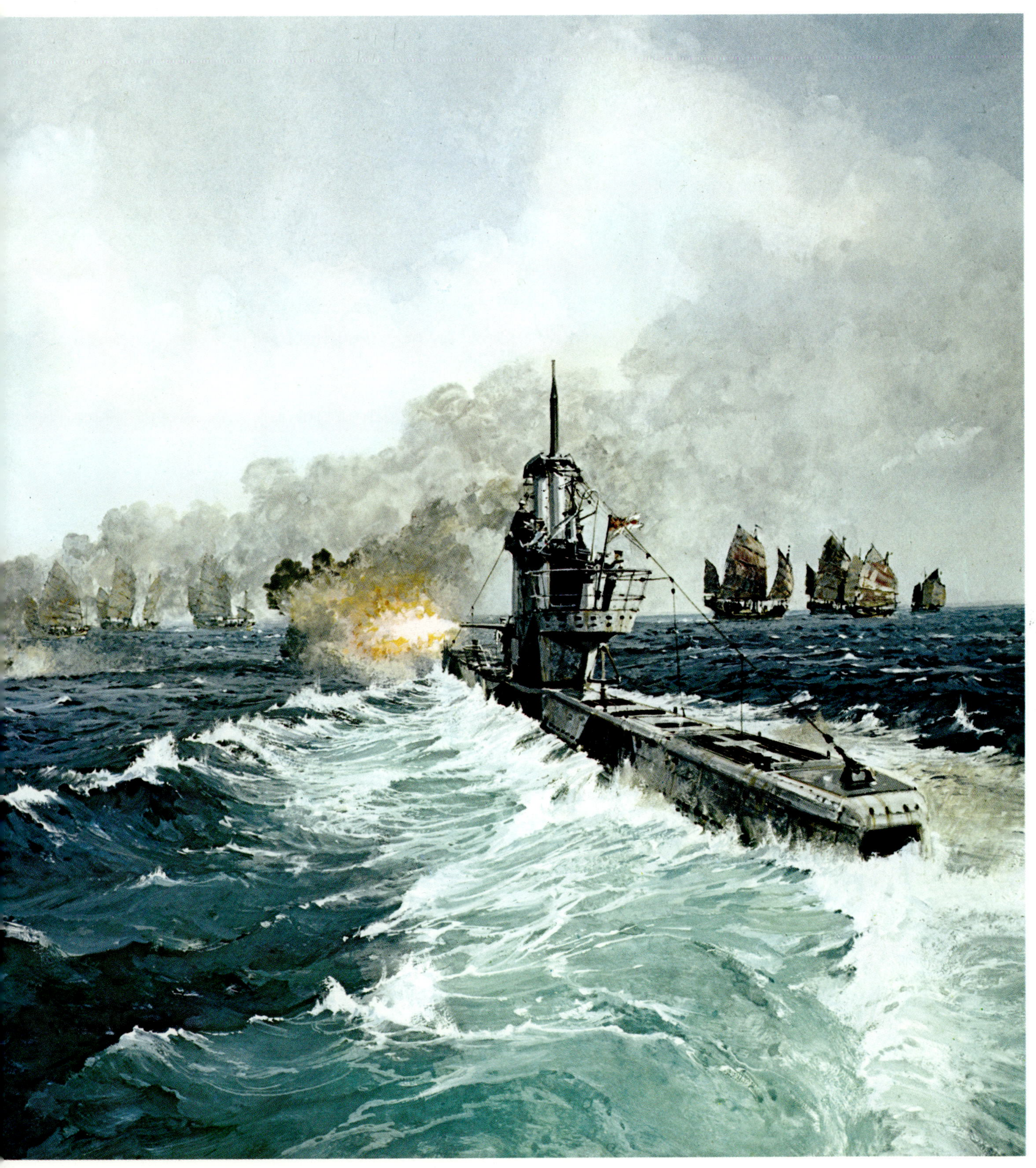

10) Sink the Tirpitz!
by Lèonce Peillard
June 1974
Mayflower/Granada Publishing

*My only reference was a diagram of the anchorage, the position
of the ship and where the bombs fell.*

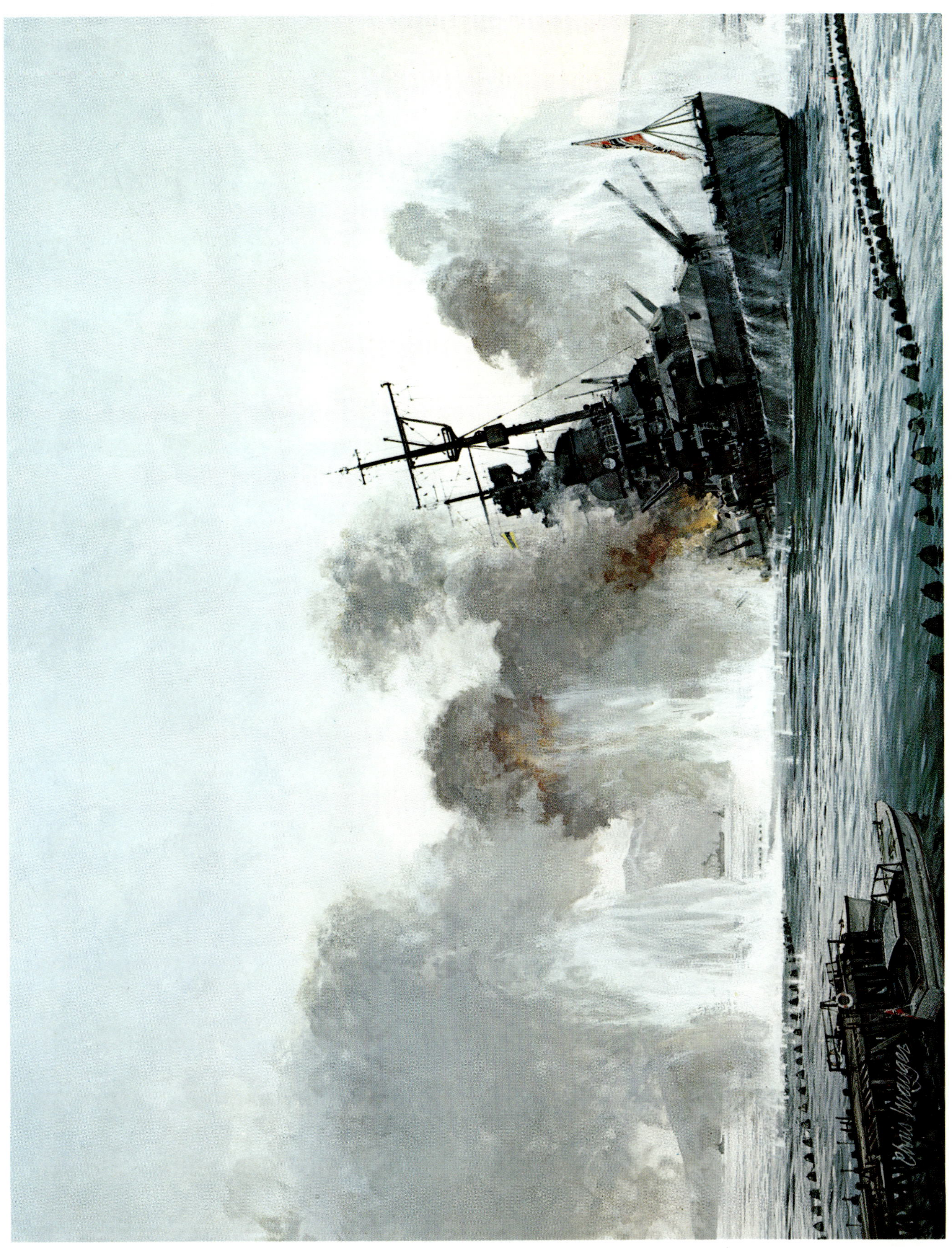

11) *Detail from*
Sink the Tirpitz!
by Lèonce Peillard
June 1974
Mayflower/Granada Publishing

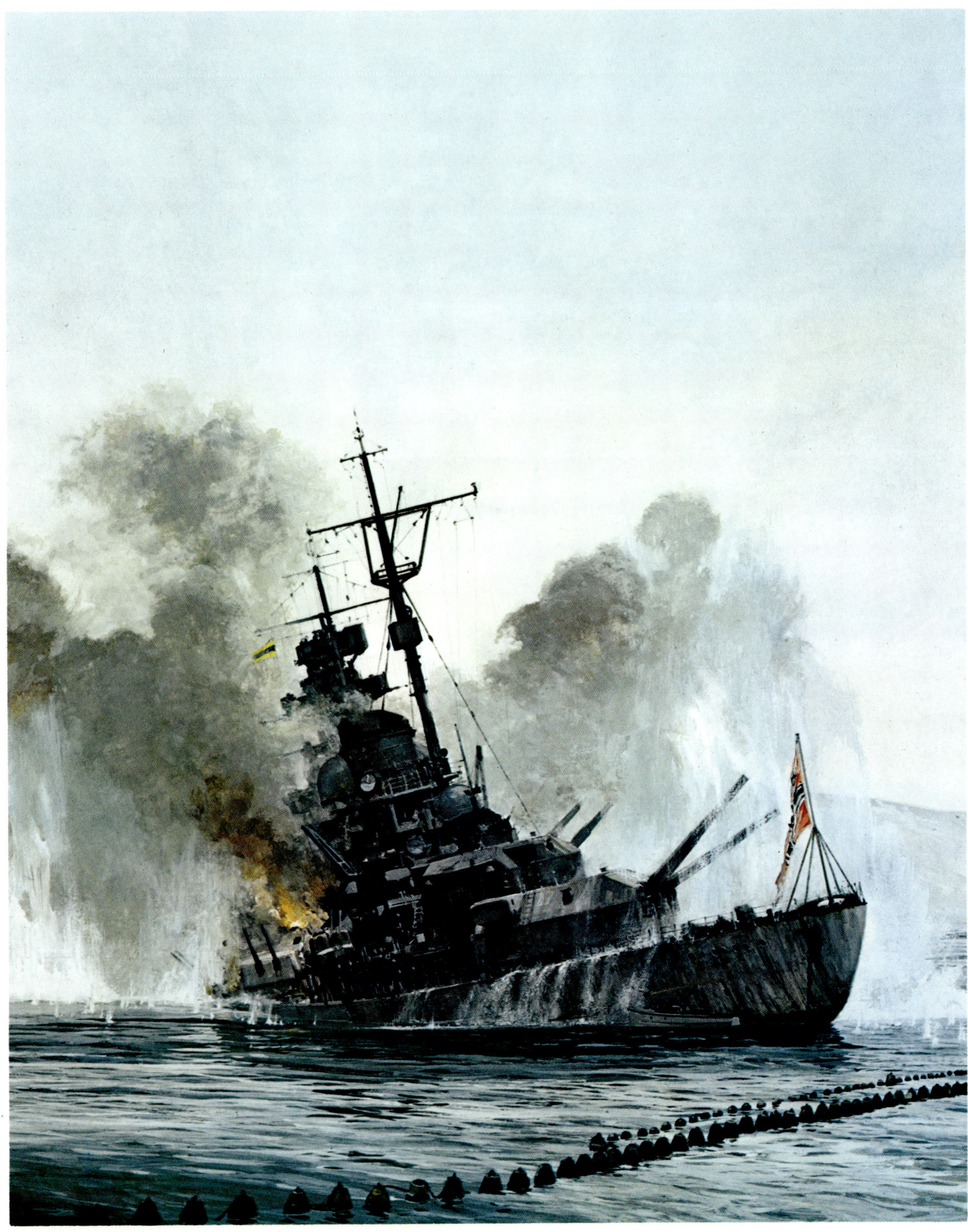

12) *Detail from*
Leviathan
by Warren Tute
January 1975
Panther/Granada Publishing
*It is difficult to imagine a ship being sunk almost entirely
by gunfire.*

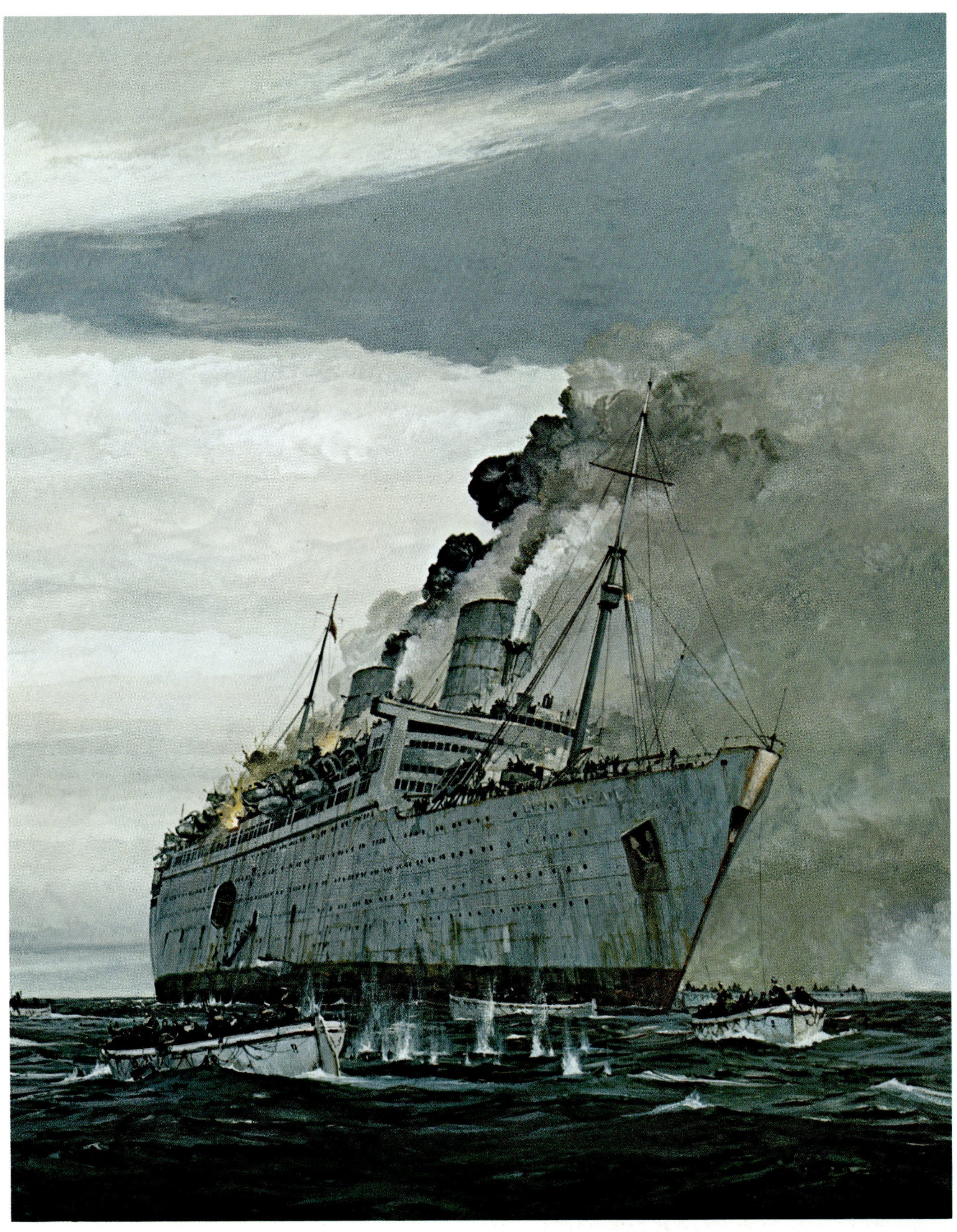

13) Pacific Ordeal
by Kenneth Ainslie
January 1975
Panther/Granada Publishing
*I only had a very poor sketch of how the sails were set to
go by on this one.*

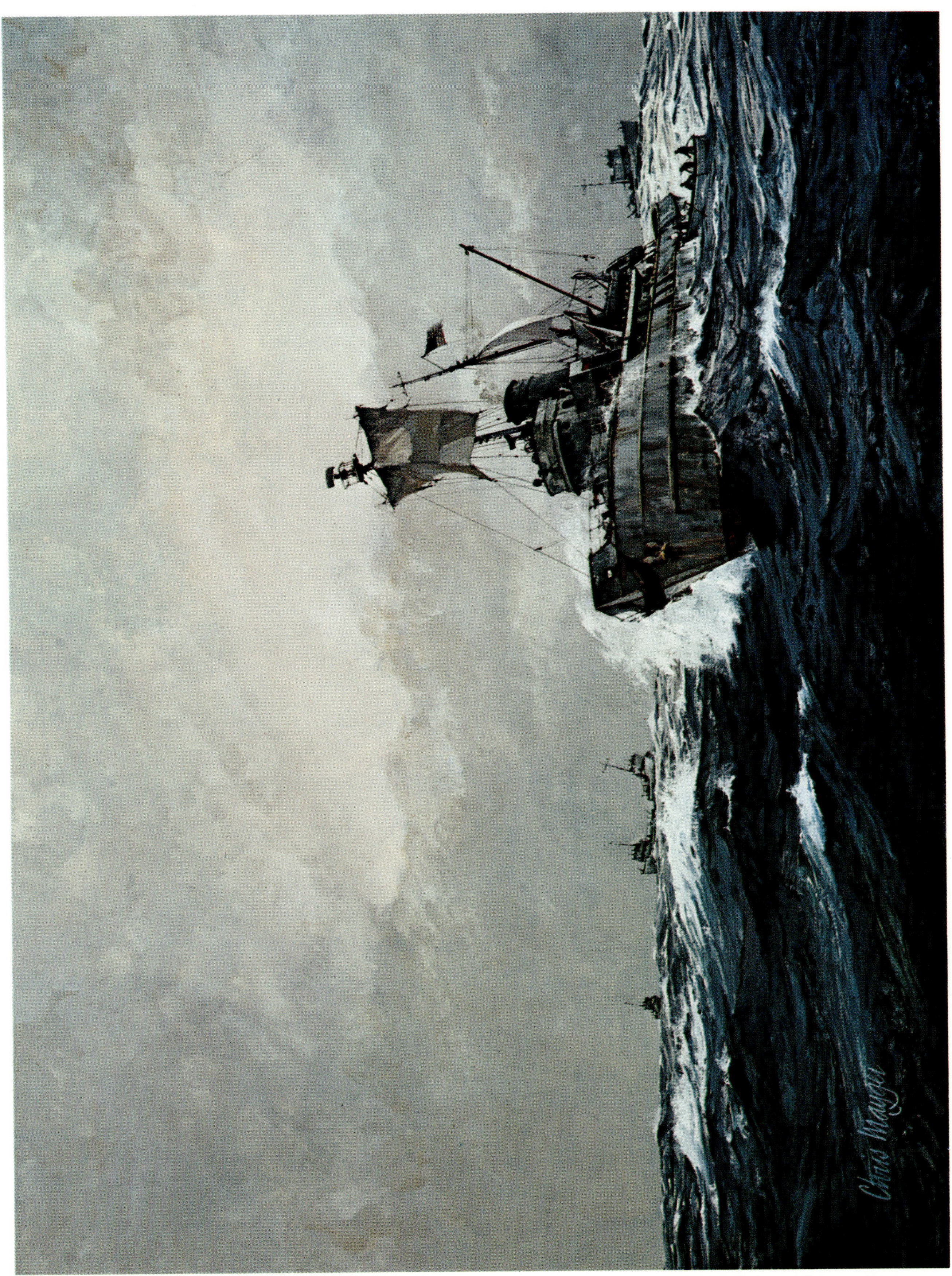

14) H.M.S. Rosemary
July 1973
Specially Commissioned
Private Collection
Mr. L. Rupert Curtis, D.S.C., F.I.P.A.
This was taken from a faded snapshot of the owner's old ship.

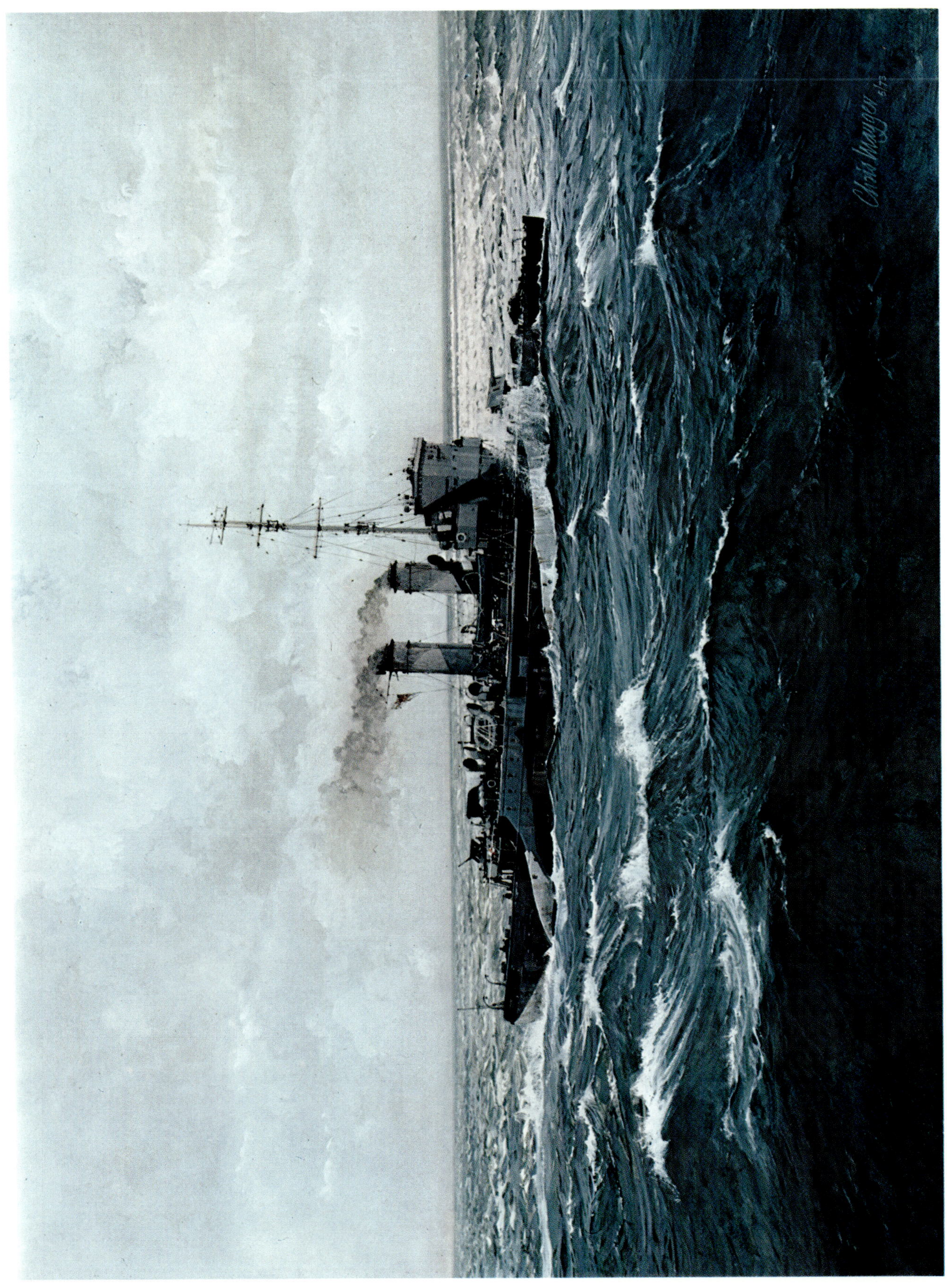

15) *Detail from*
Cornish Shipwrecks – The South Coast
by Richard Larn and Clive Carter
August 1972
Pan Books

Based on the wreck of the Andola in 1895 on Shark Fin Rock.

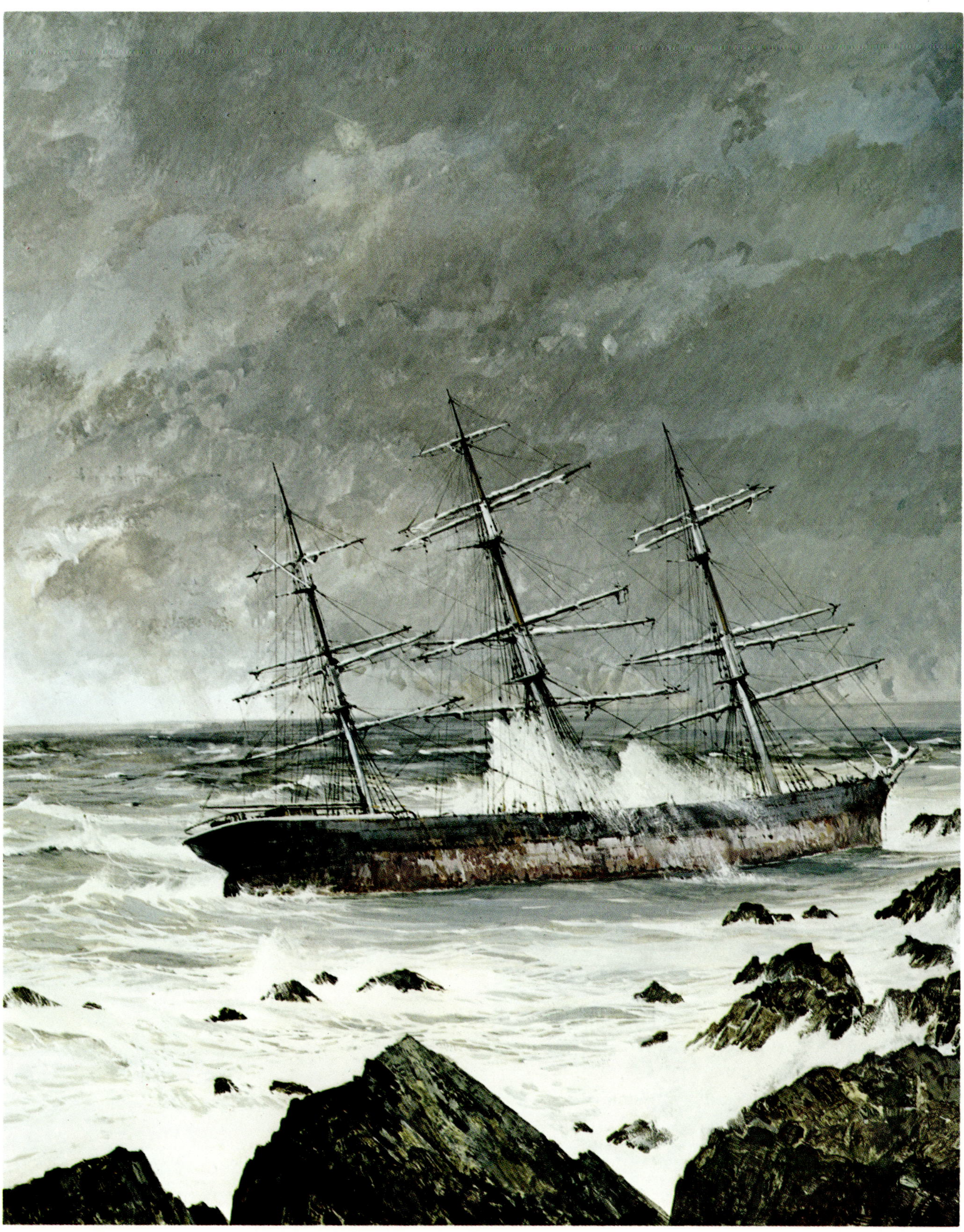

I've received letters from admirers on this one.

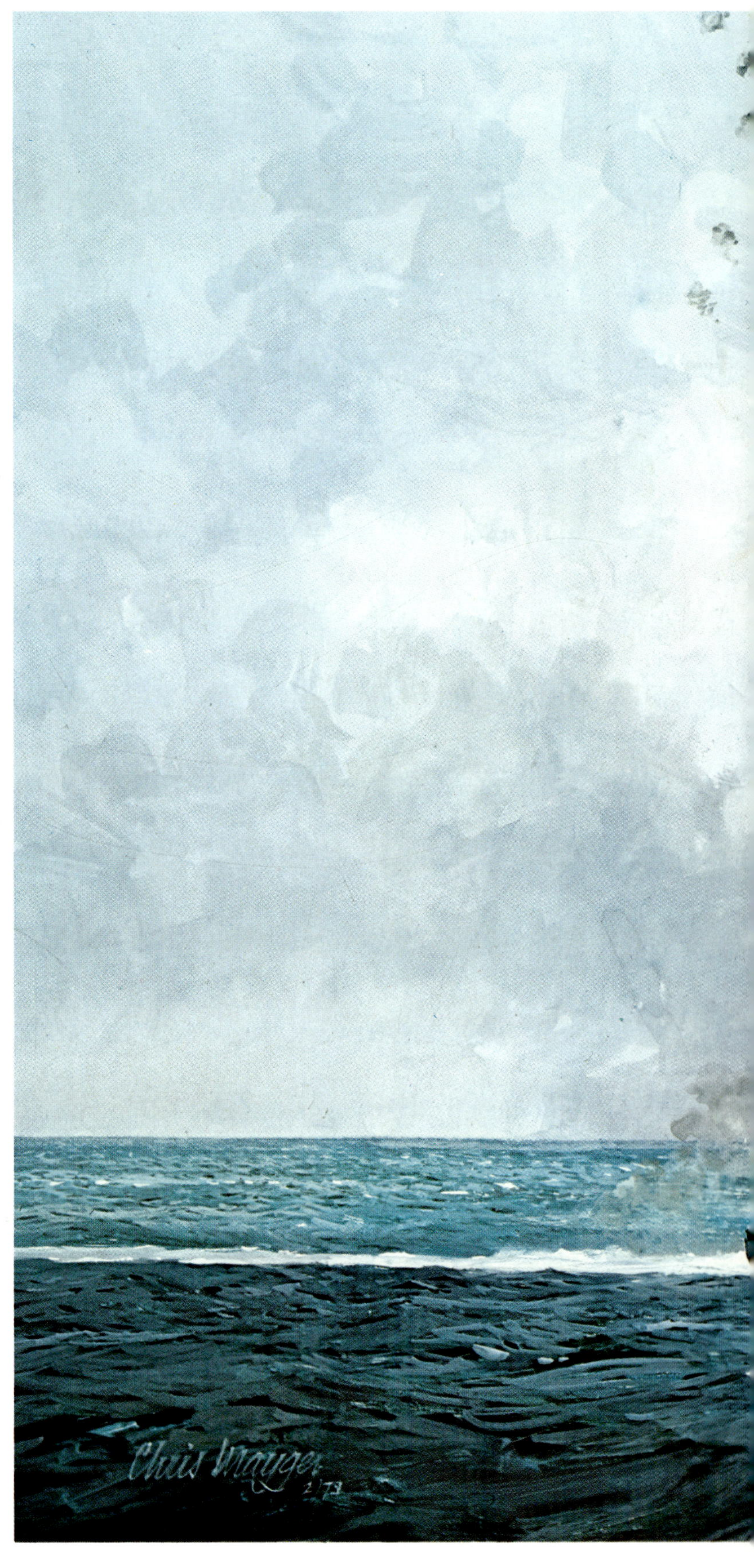

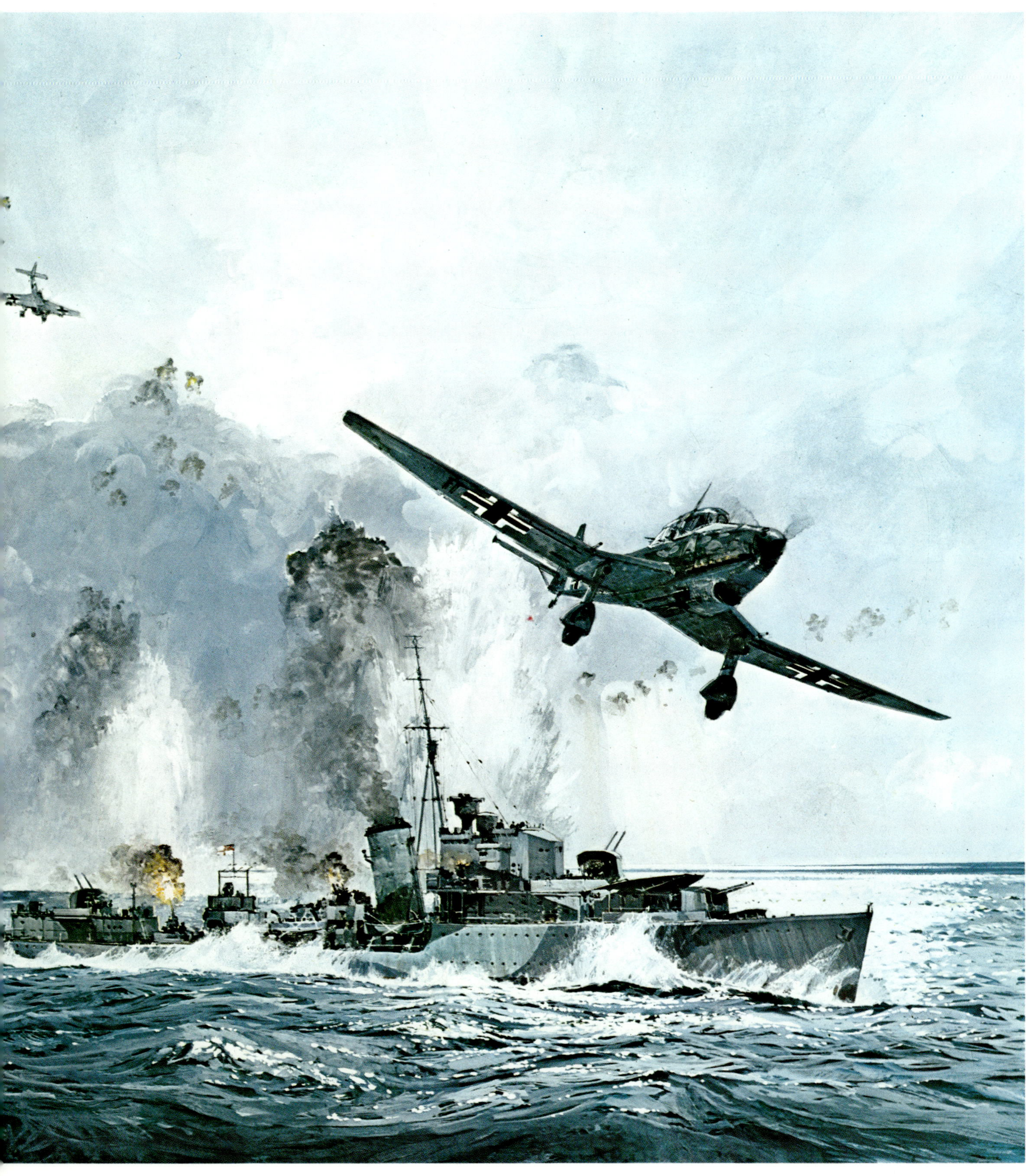

17) The Ship That Saved Malta
by George Pollock
October 1973
Reader's Digest Magazine

*This had to be done in three days. I only had an aerial view
of the disabled ship being towed into Malta as reference.*

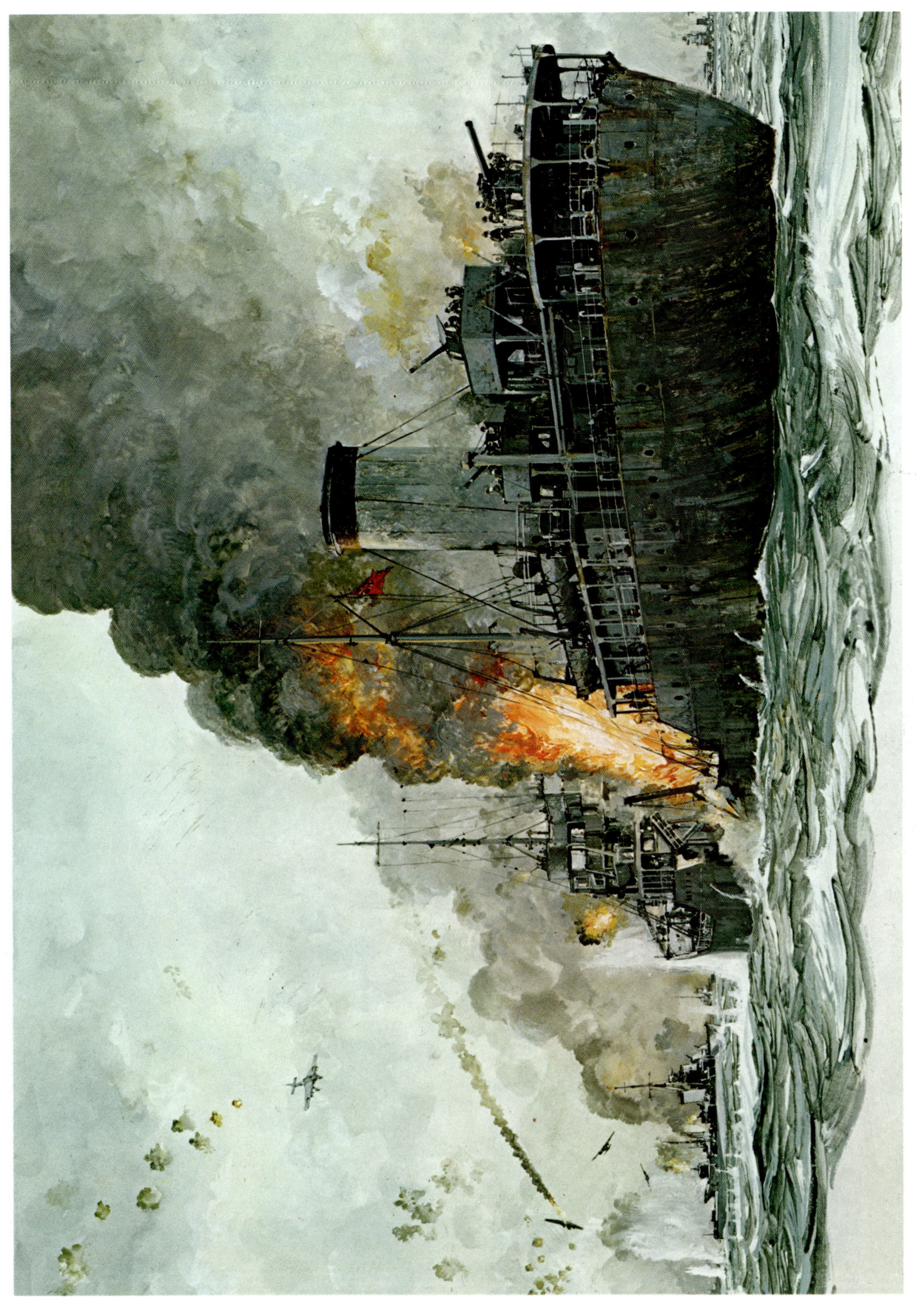

18) Rendezvous South Atlantic
by Douglas Reeman
August 1971
Reader's Digest Condensed Books

". . . probably a liner, with two funnels and a large
Swedish Flag painted on her side." – *It is very foggy and
the two men in the bows hear only a scraping of metal as the
false bridge is being lifted. On this job I painted the fog first
and then painted the detail into it.*

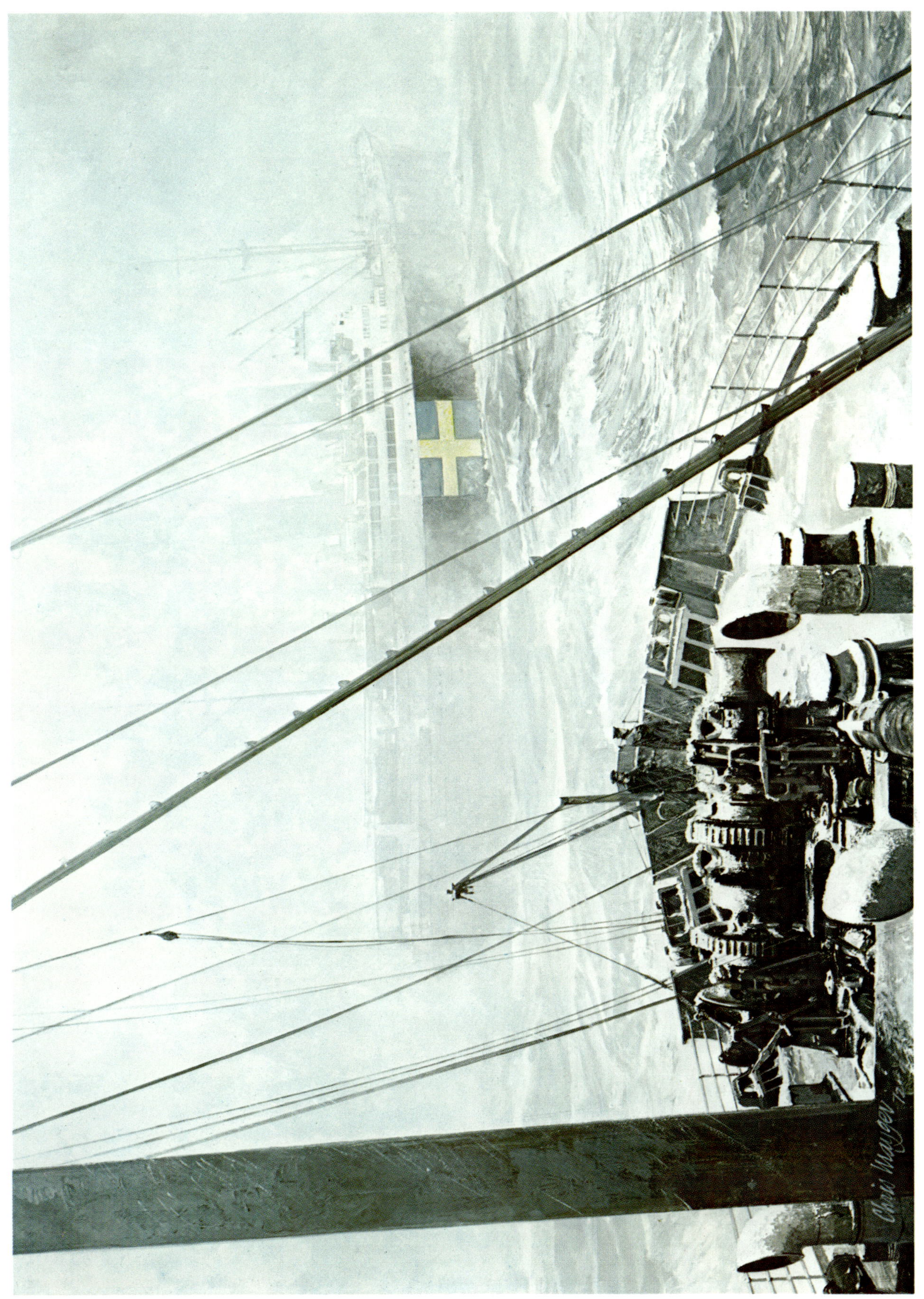

19) Grey Wolf, Grey Sea
by E. B. Gasaway
June 1974
Futura Publications Ltd.

*I tried to capture the loneliness of a solitary submarine waiting
for its prey in an empty sea.*

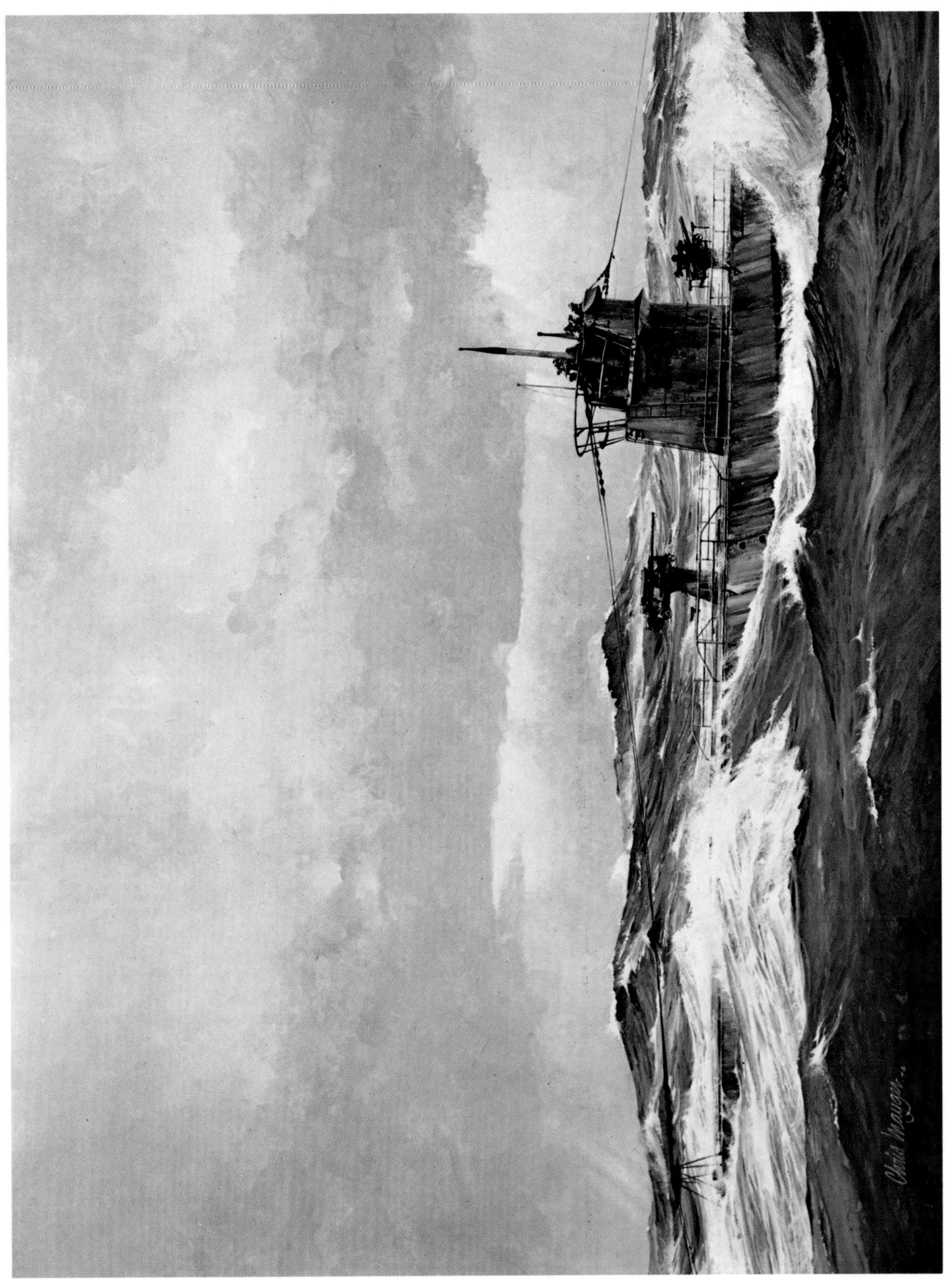

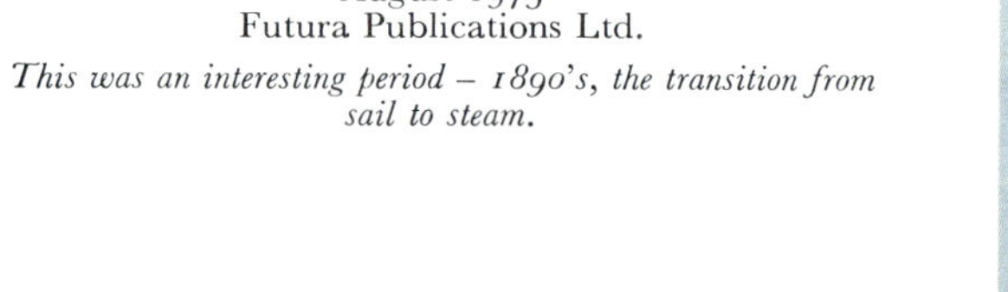

20) Beware the Bight of Benin
by Philip McCutchan
August 1975
Futura Publications Ltd.

*This was an interesting period – 1890's, the transition from
sail to steam.*

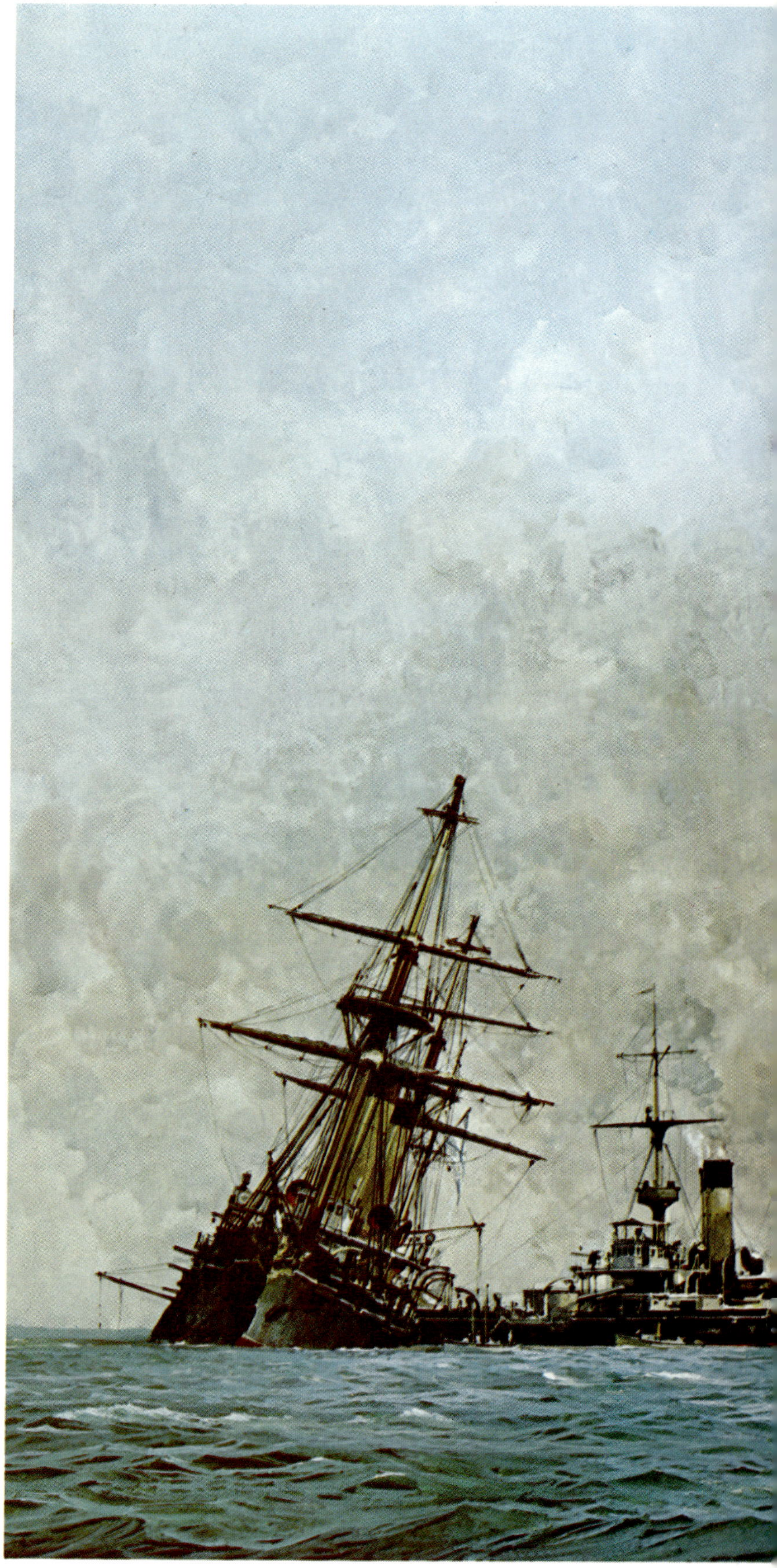

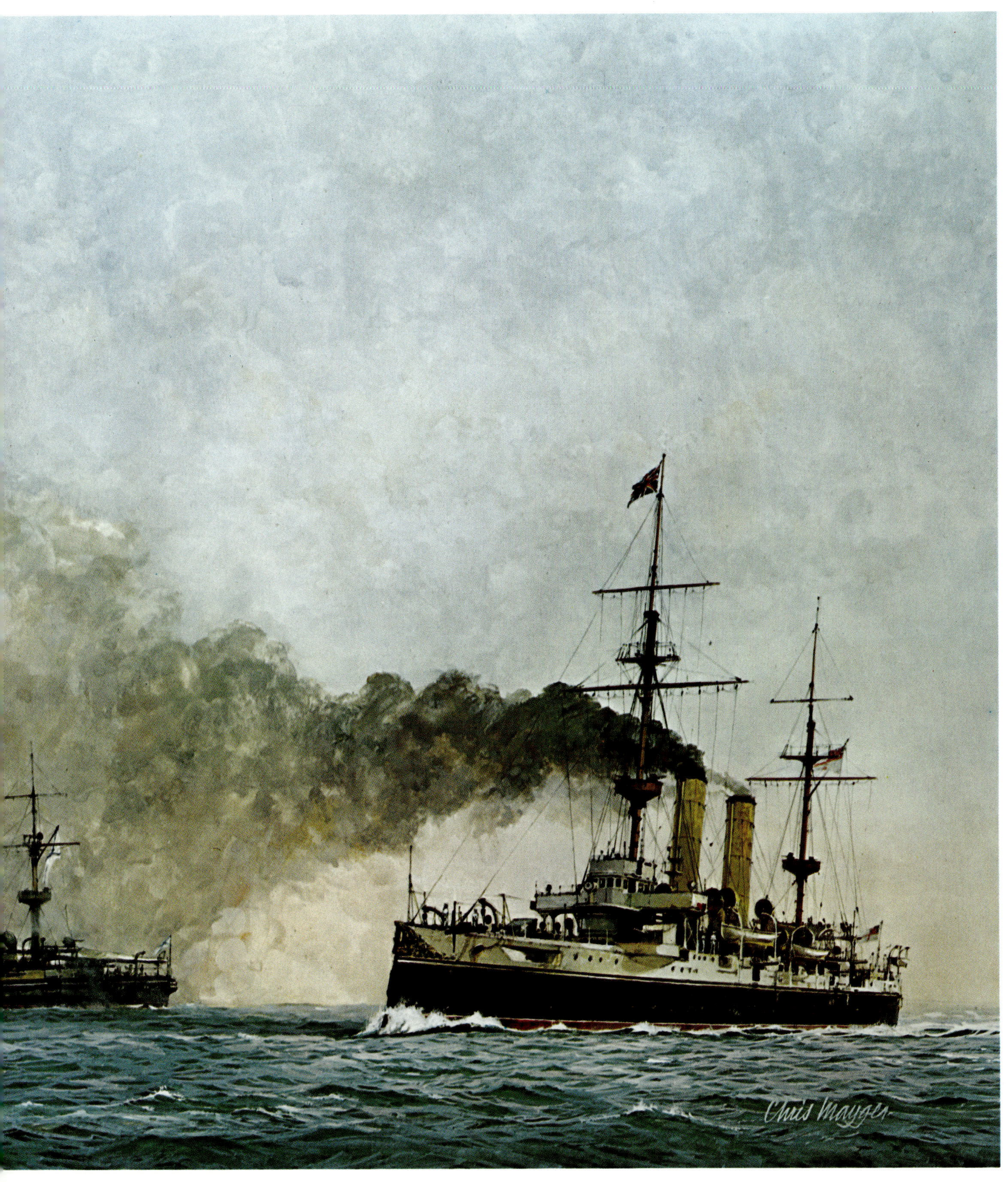

Chris Mayger

21) The Clippers
by Kenneth Cook
August 1975
Futura Publications Ltd.

*Difficult, because I feel that Clippers have been exploited and
also because I didn't have the book to read before I did the
painting.*

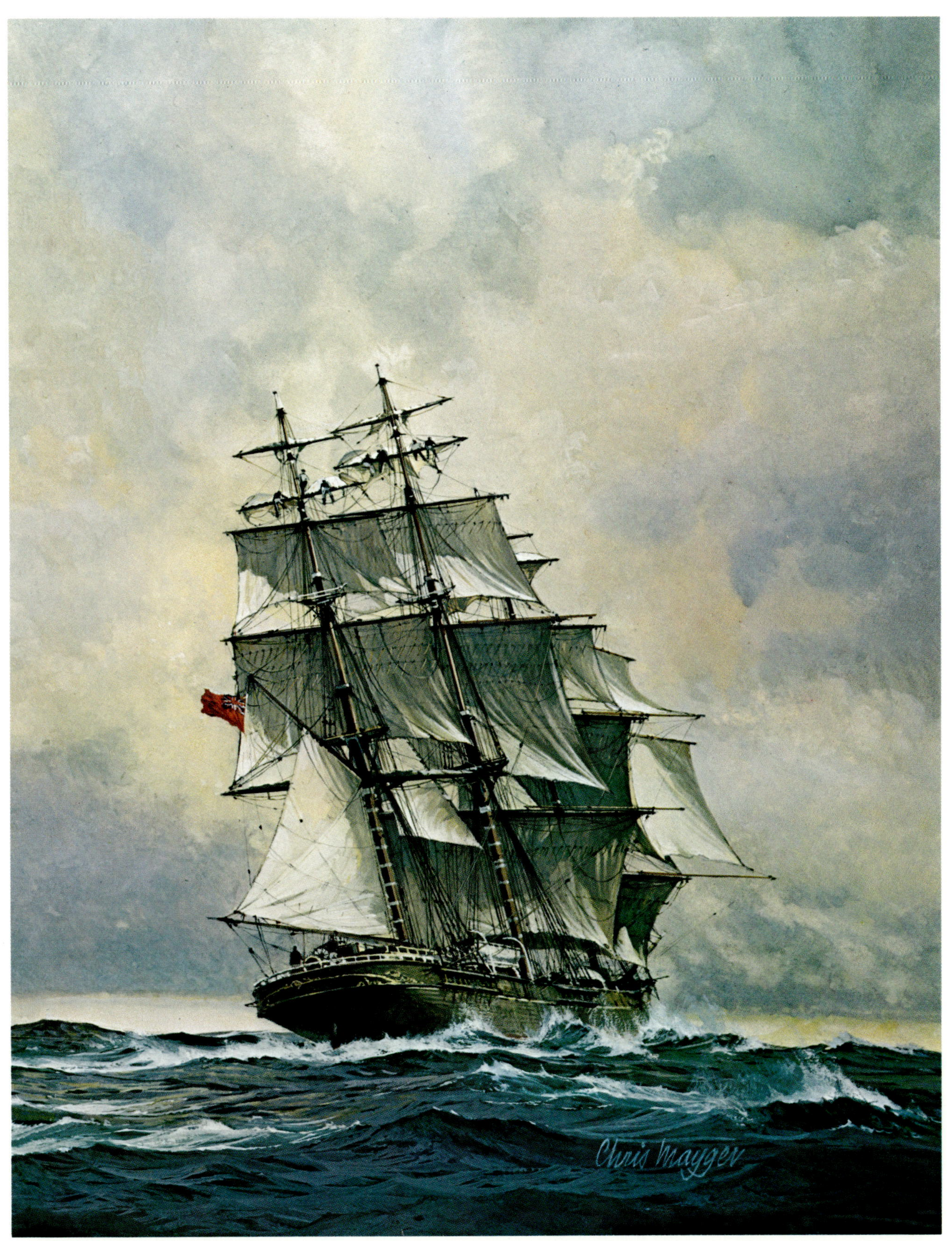

Chris Mayger

22) Destroyers One
The Flotilla Attack
by Duncan Harding
October 1975
Futura Publications Ltd.

*This is an odd ship of outsize
tonnage and there was no
reference, it is the only one in the
Royal Navy.*

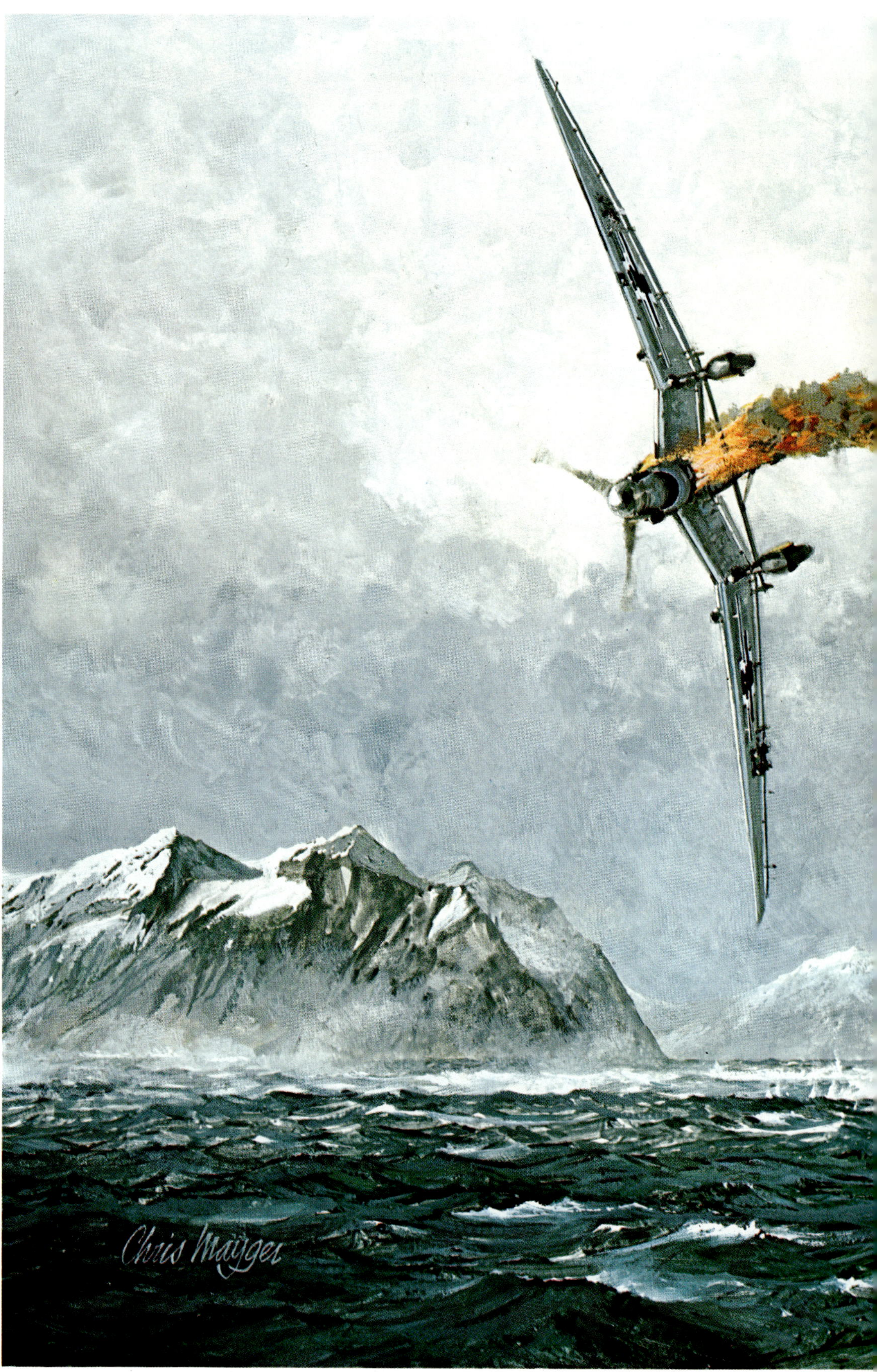

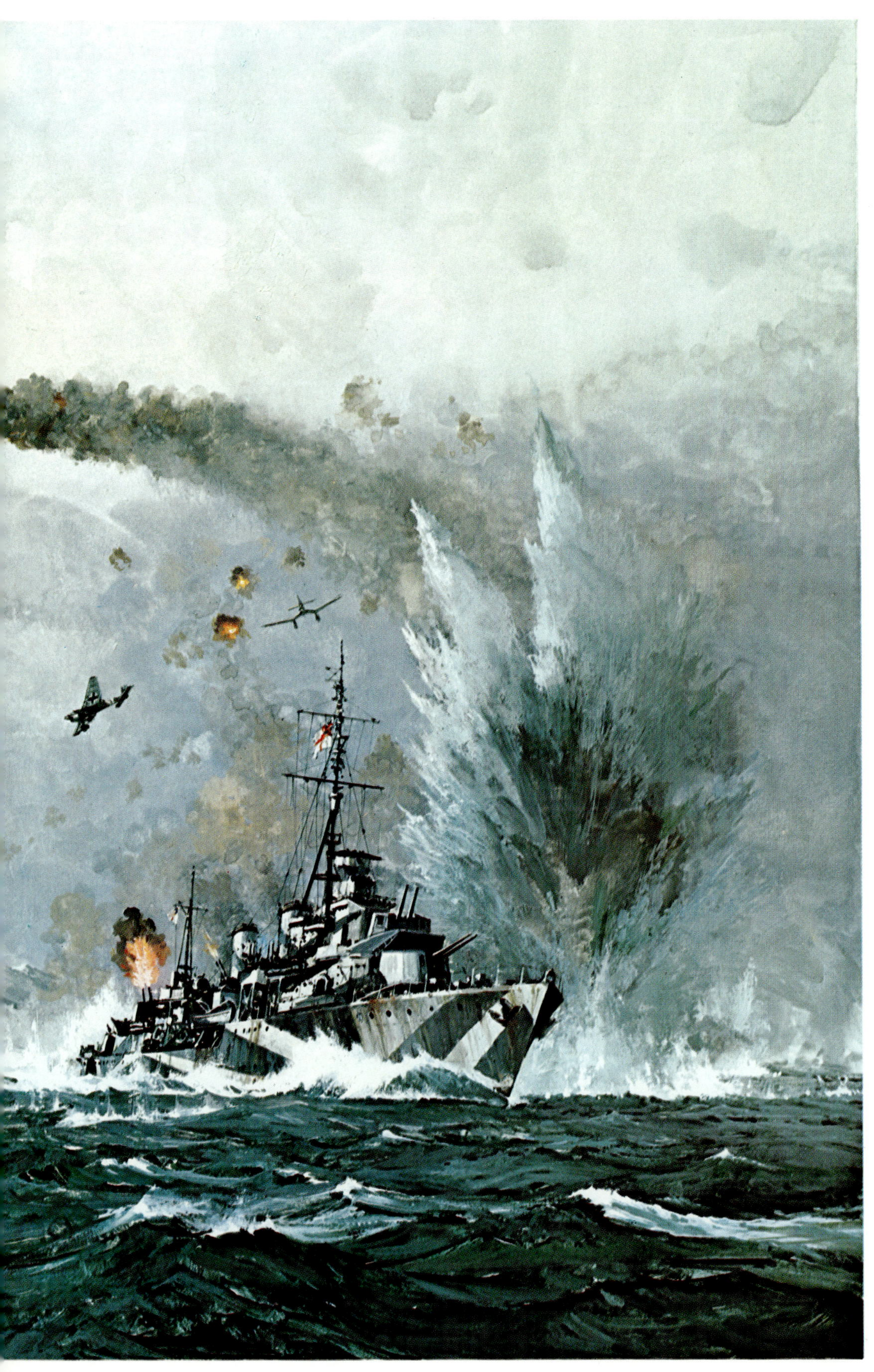

23) The Serpent's Coil
by Farley Mowat
March 1973
Ballantine Books
A nice straightforward job, good Author's description.

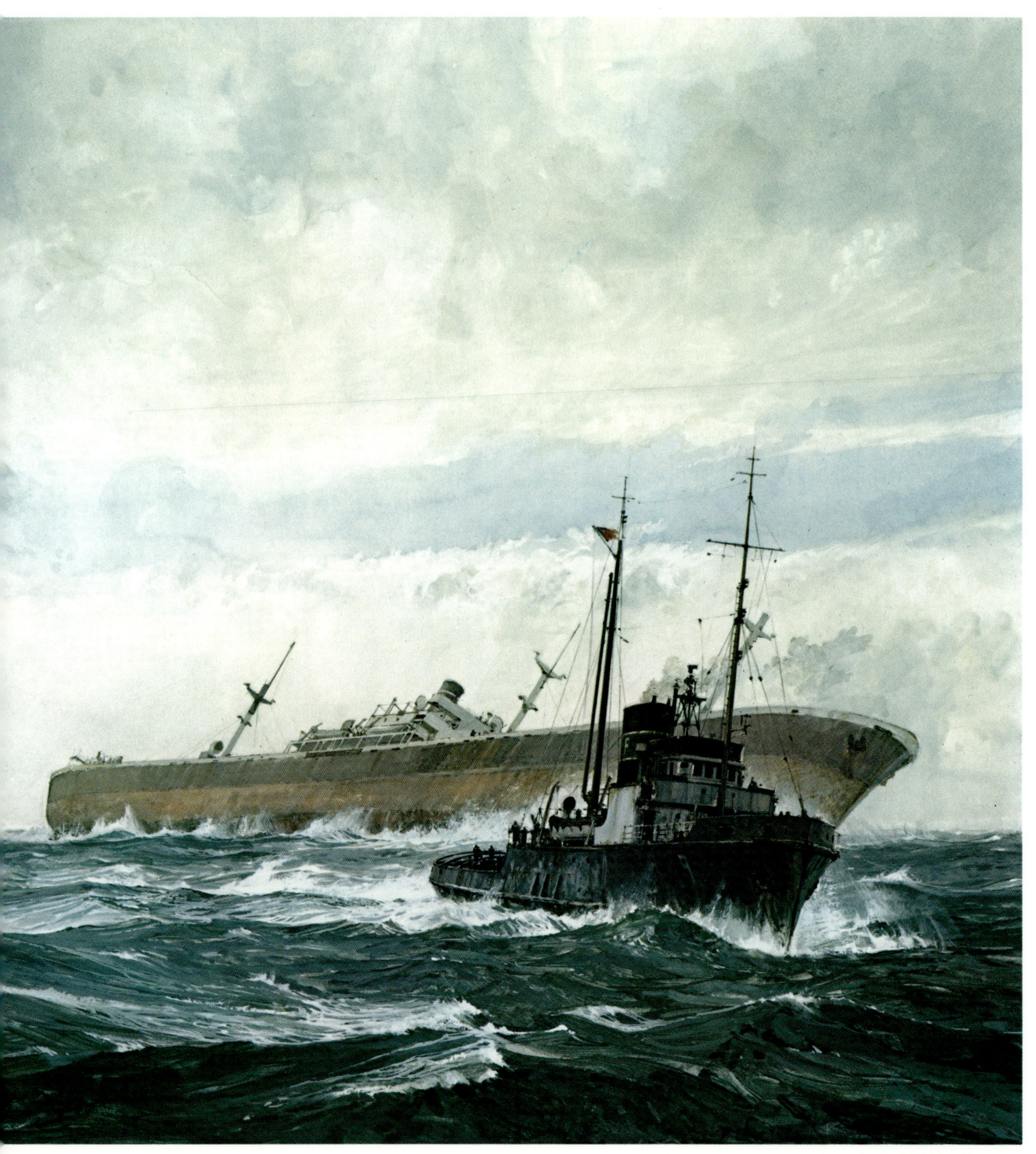

24) The Defeat of John Hawkins
by Rayner Unwin
April 1973
Ballantine Books

*The Author gives an excellent description of life at sea. I had
to try and make the galleon look real and not like a model,
there is little reference for Tudor ships.*

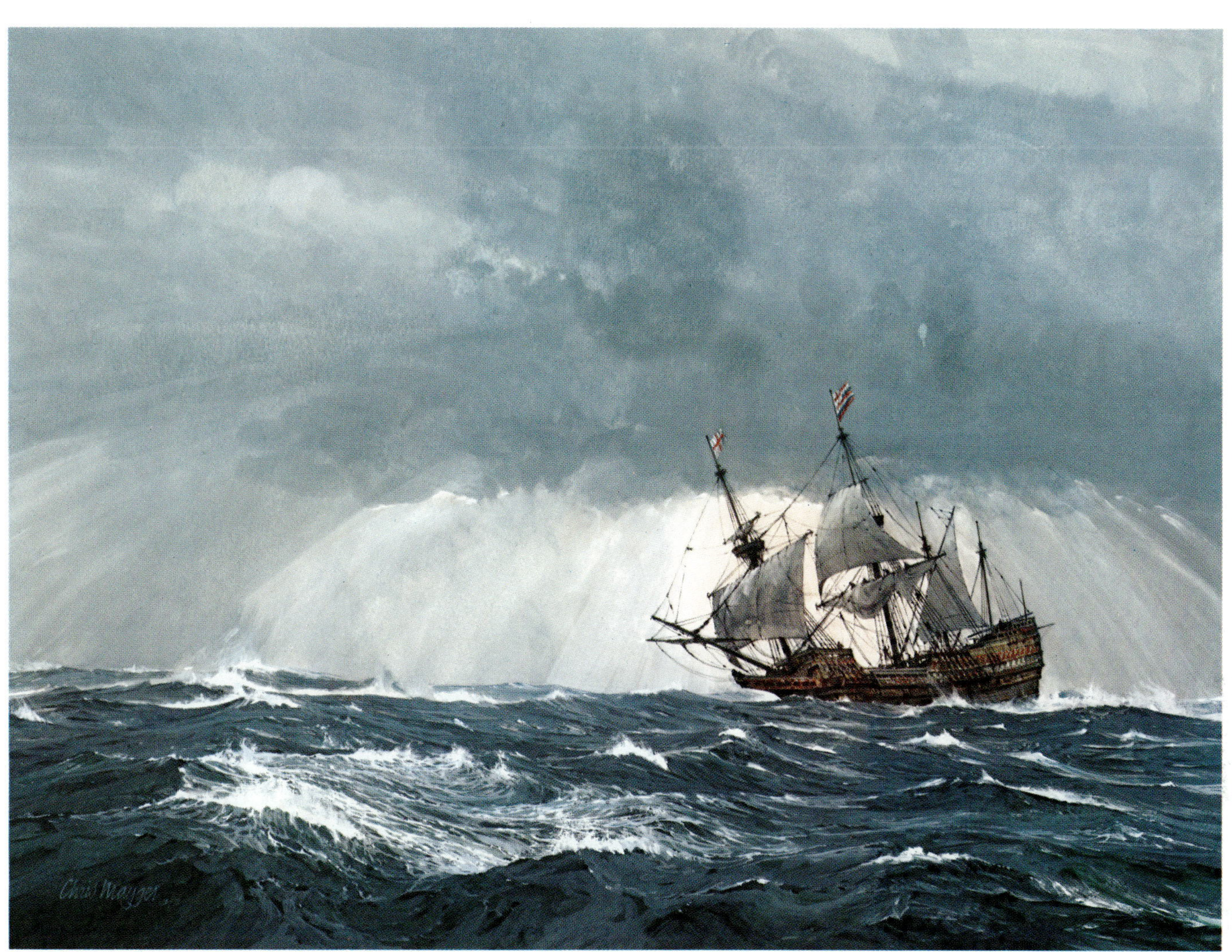

25) *Detail from*
The Defeat of John Hawkins
by Rayner Unwin
April 1973
Ballantine Books

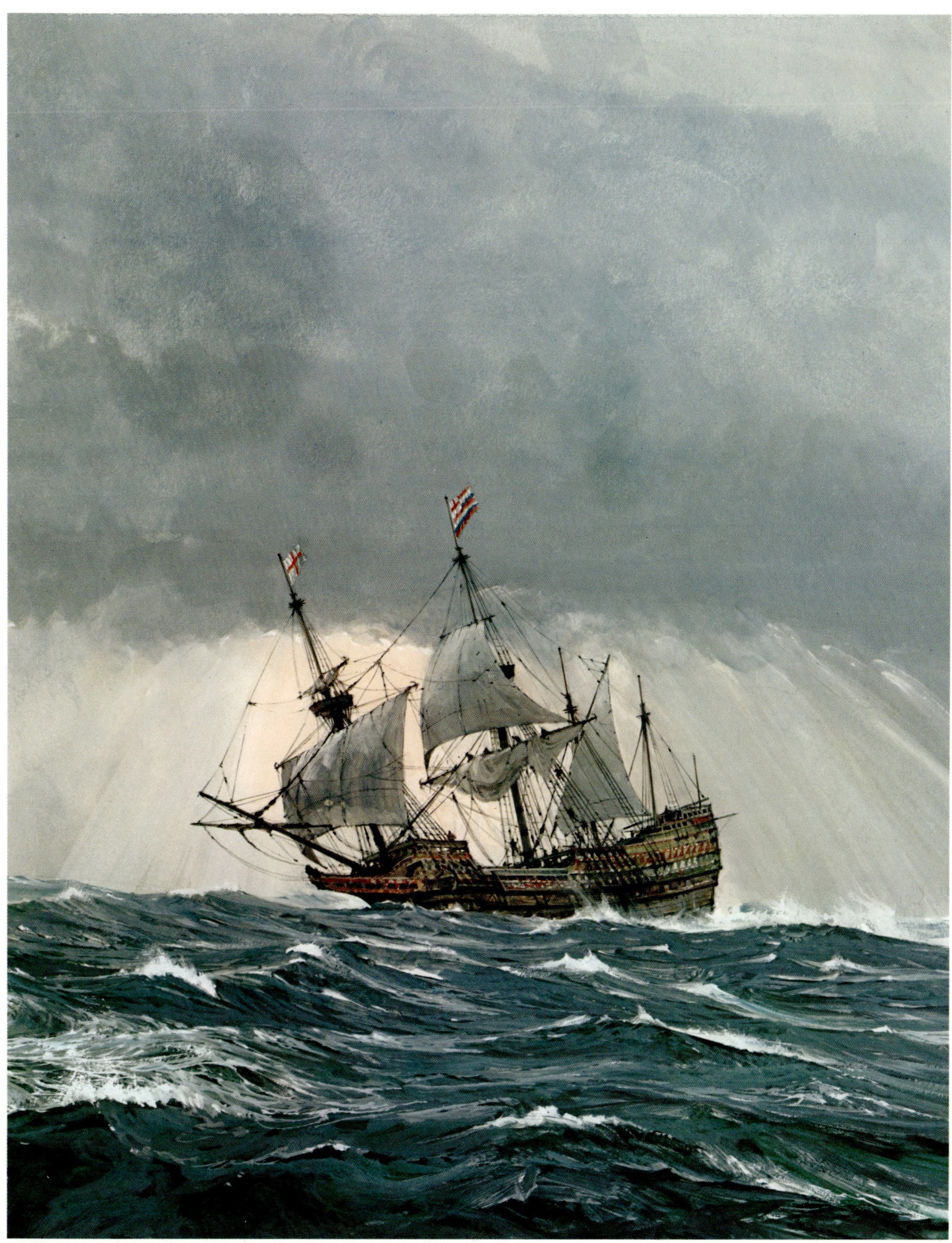

26) Grey Seas Under
by Farley Mowat
April 1973
Ballantine Books

*This is a converted, British, ex-naval tug – there was very
little reference other than a diagram in the book.*

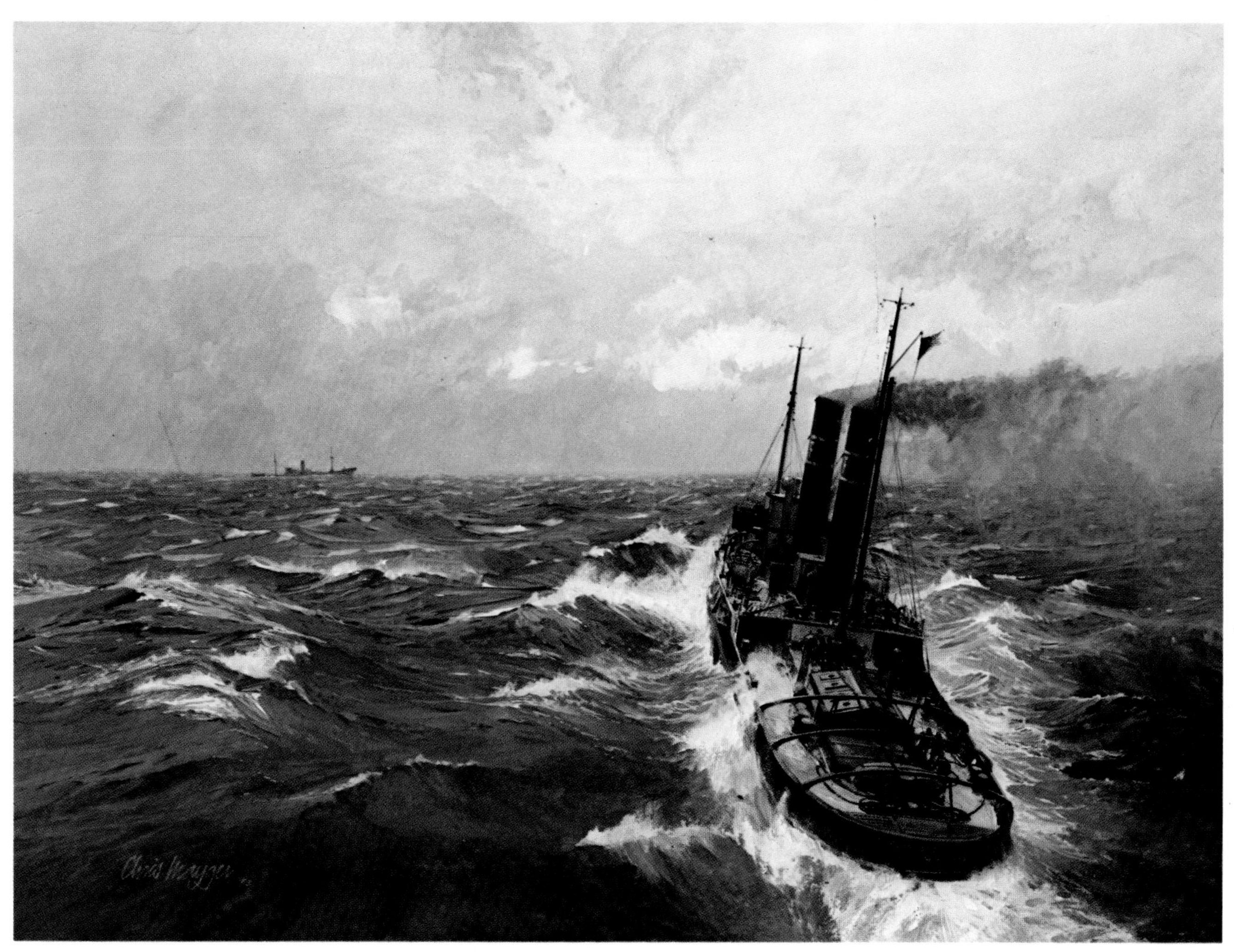

27) *Detail from*
Grey Seas Under
by Farley Mowat
April 1973
Ballantine Books

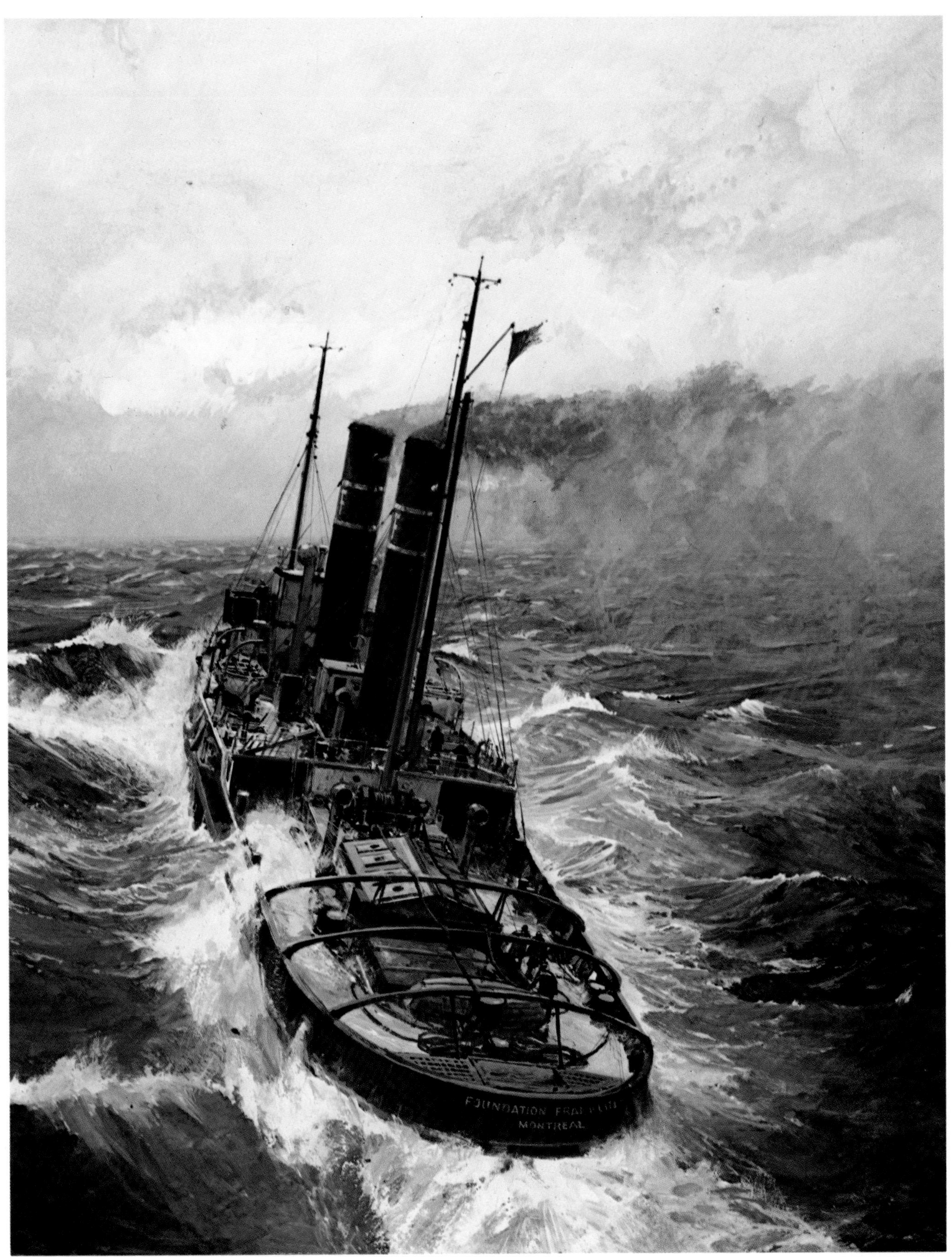

FOUNDATION FRANKLIN
MONTREAL

28) The Prospect of Whitby – 1939
September 1973
Specially Commissioned
Private Collection
Mr. R. J. Lovell, F.I.P.A.

*This Thames-side pub has completely changed in 30-odd years
and I was stumped until a member of the London Fire Service
produced a 35-year-old, 35mm transparency.*

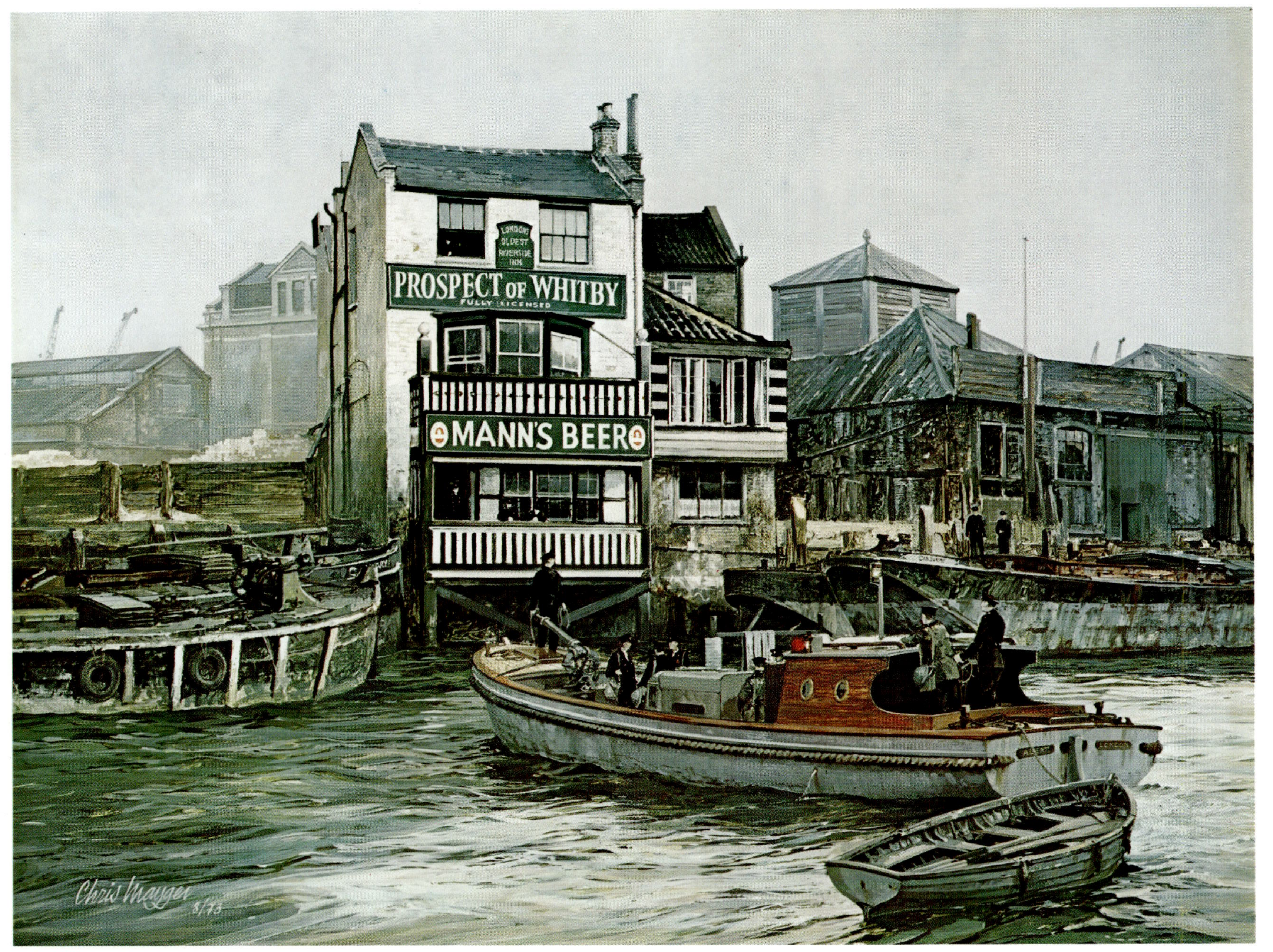

LONDON'S
OLDEST
RIVERSIDE
INN
PROSPECT OF WHITBY
FULLY LICENSED
MANN'S BEER
Chris Mayger
8/73

29) Captain Bligh and Mr. Christian
The Mutiny
by Richard Hough
September 1972
Reader's Digest Condensed Books

*Taken from another painting, but brought up to date and made
more accurate.*

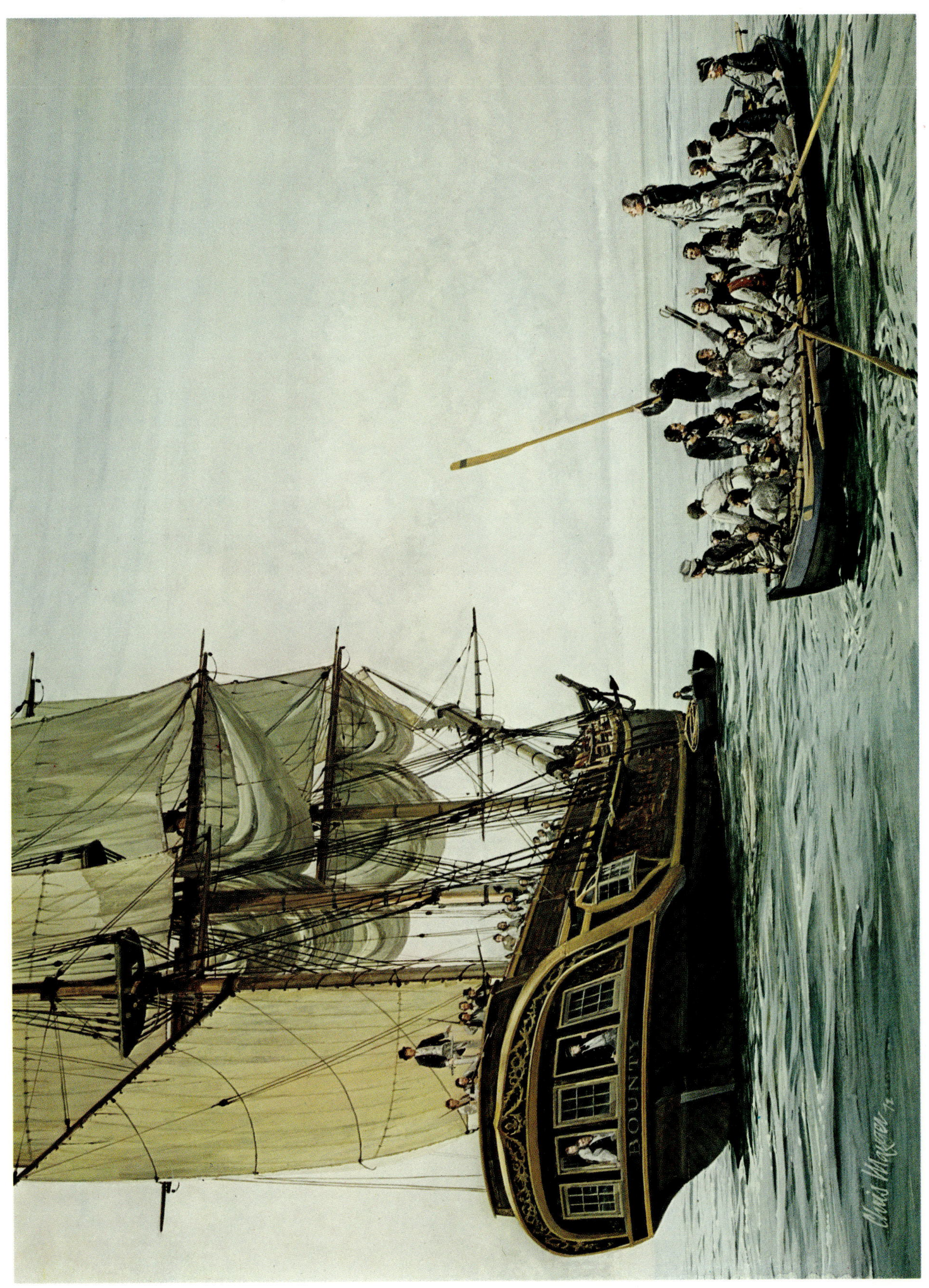

30) Captain Bligh and Mr. Christian
Cook's Anchorage, Tahiti
by Richard Hough
September 1972
Reader's Digest Condensed Books

*It took a lot of research getting this right, where the sun rose,
etc. A cousin who visited Australia told me about the black sand.*

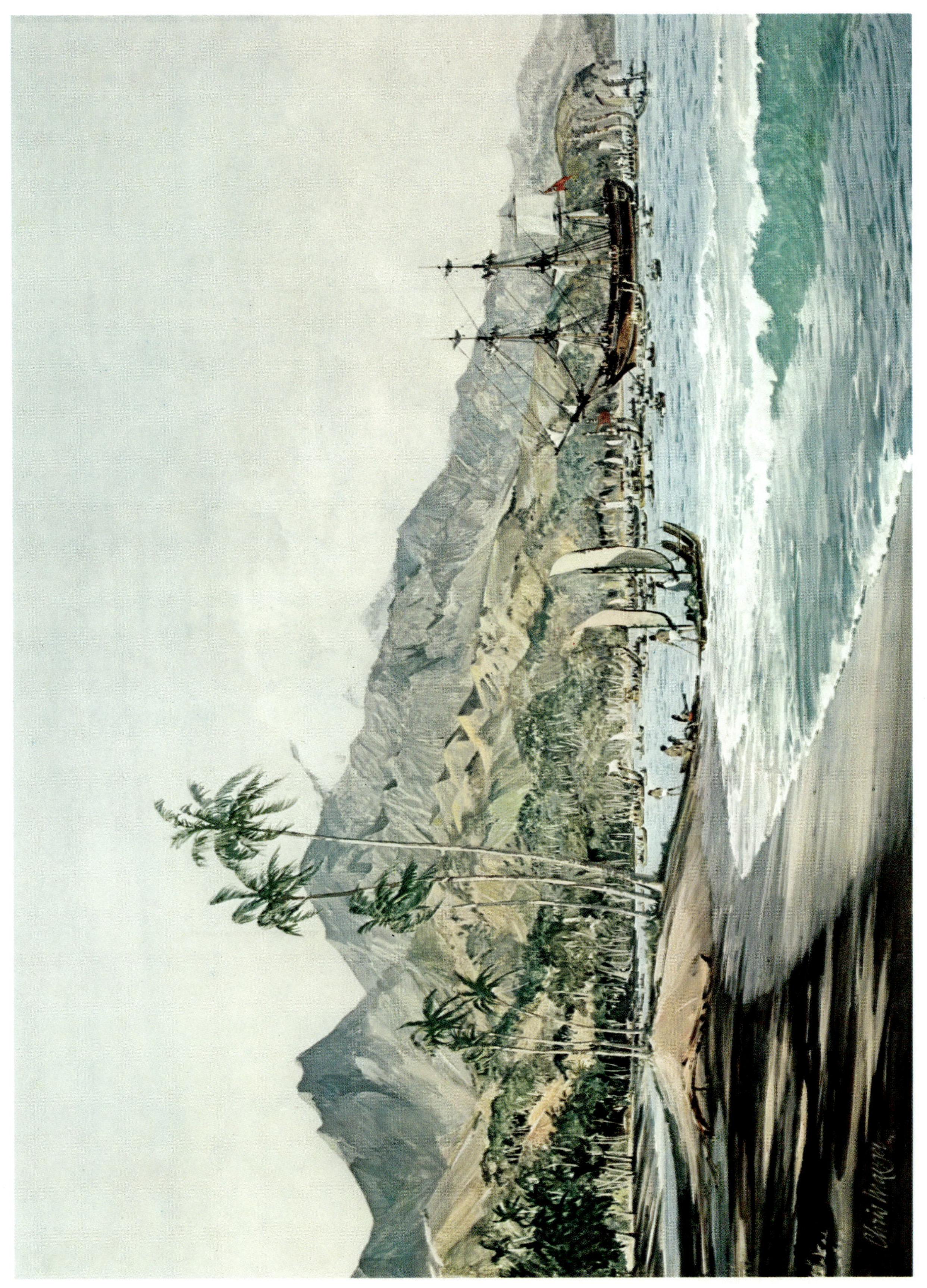

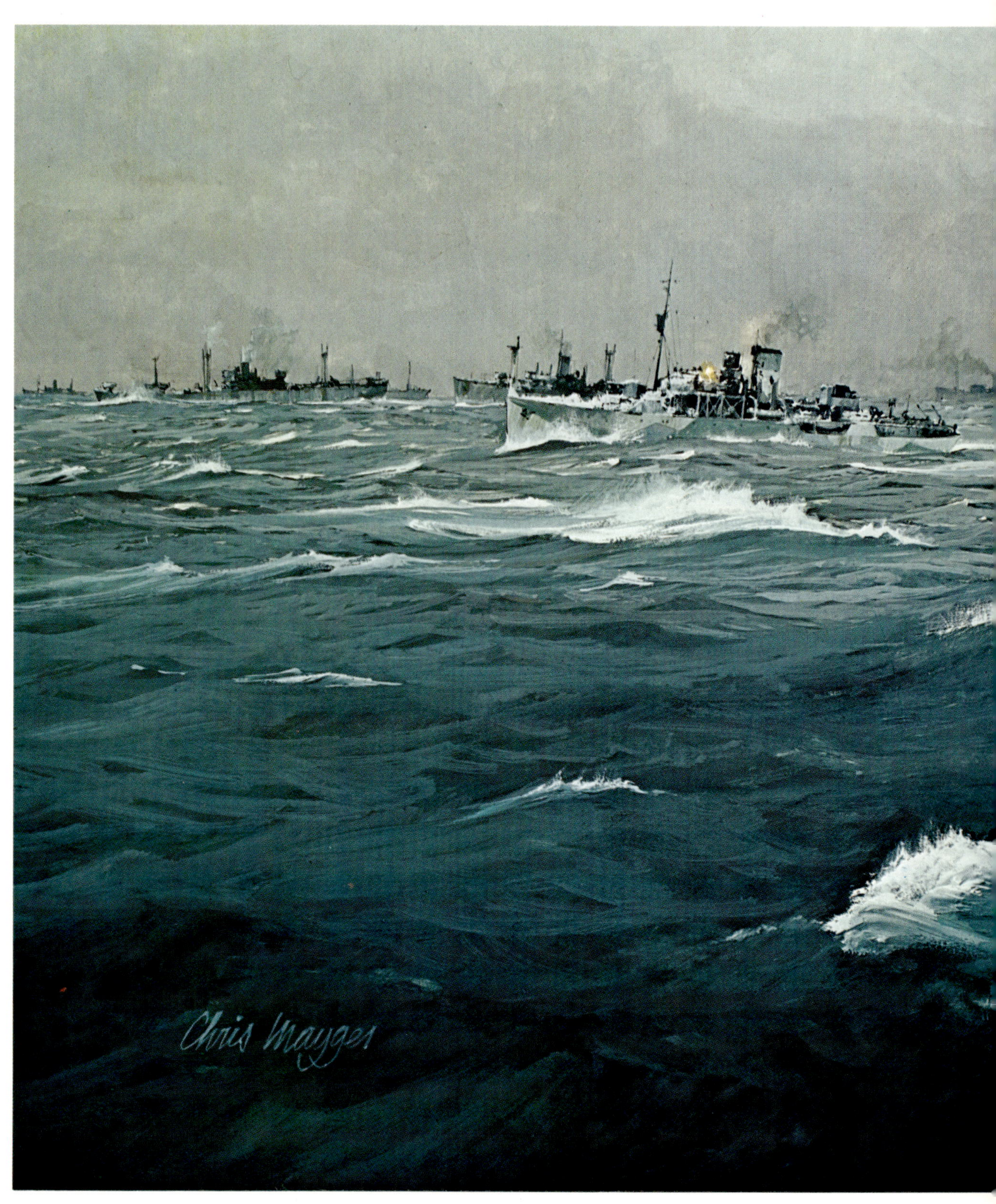

31) The Kola Run, by Ian Campbell, August 1974, Futura Publications Ltd.
It is difficult making ships appear real when encased in ice.

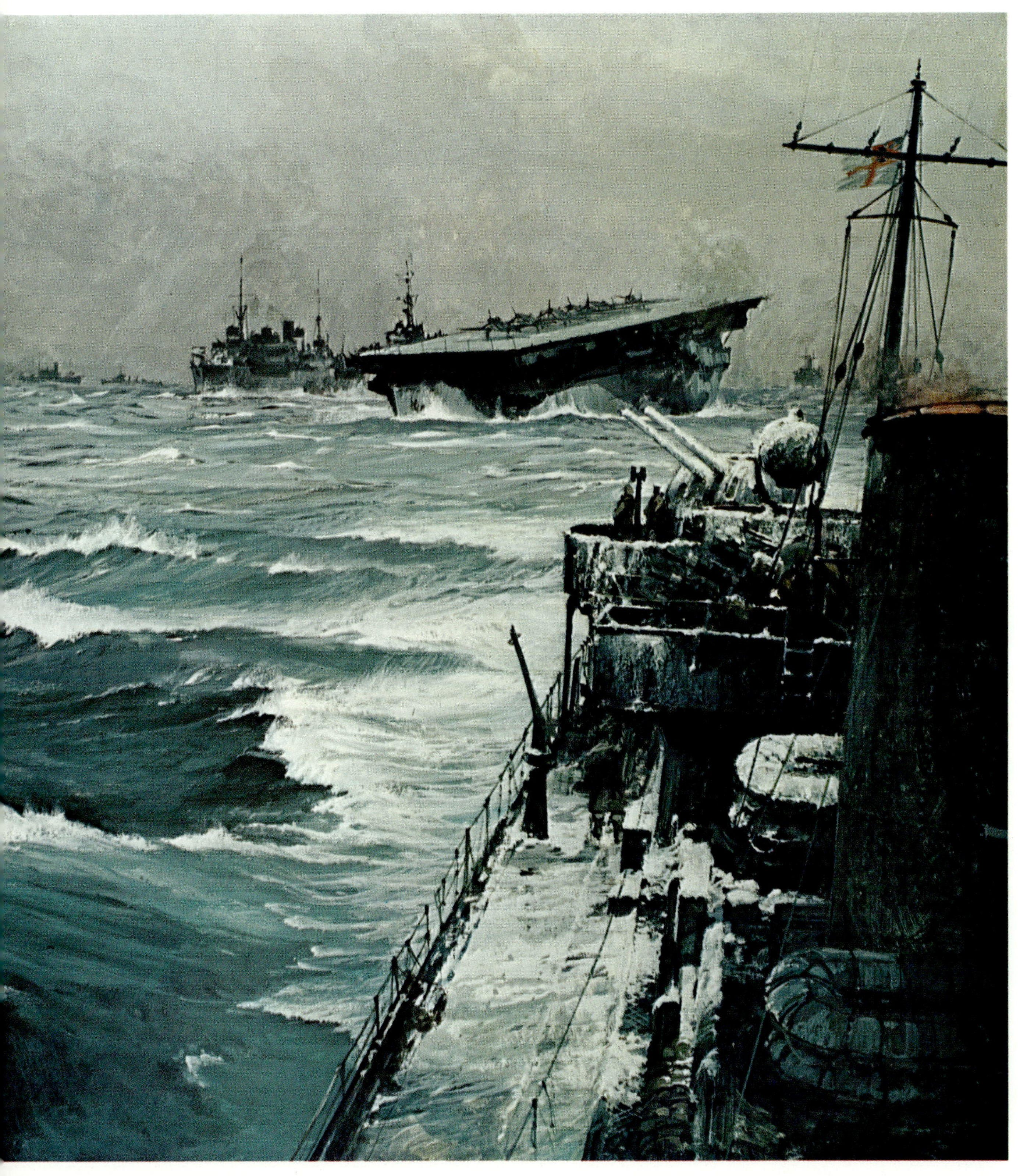

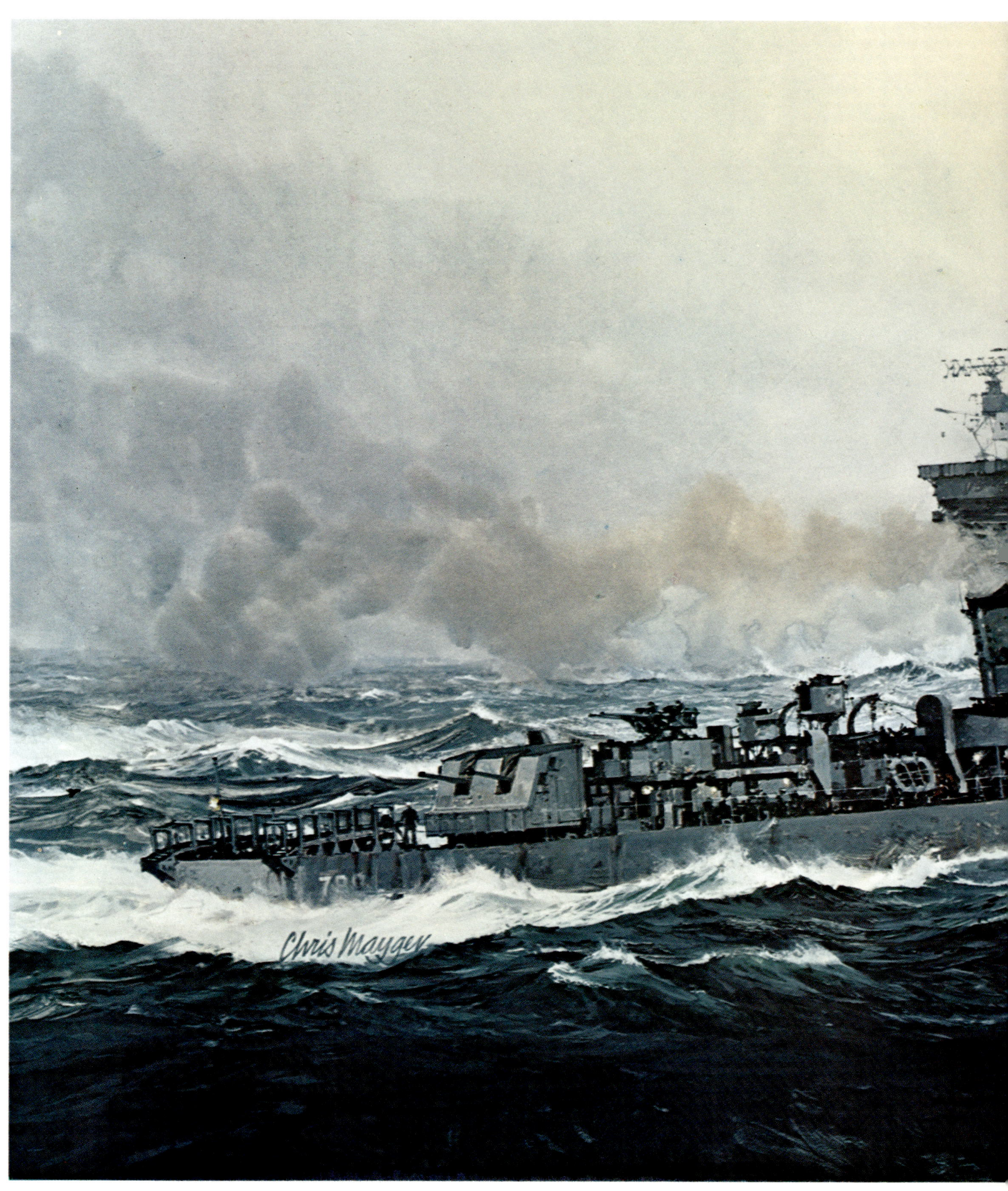

32) The Truxton Cipher, by Henry Gruppe, October 1975, Coronet Books
This really worked well in a very short time.

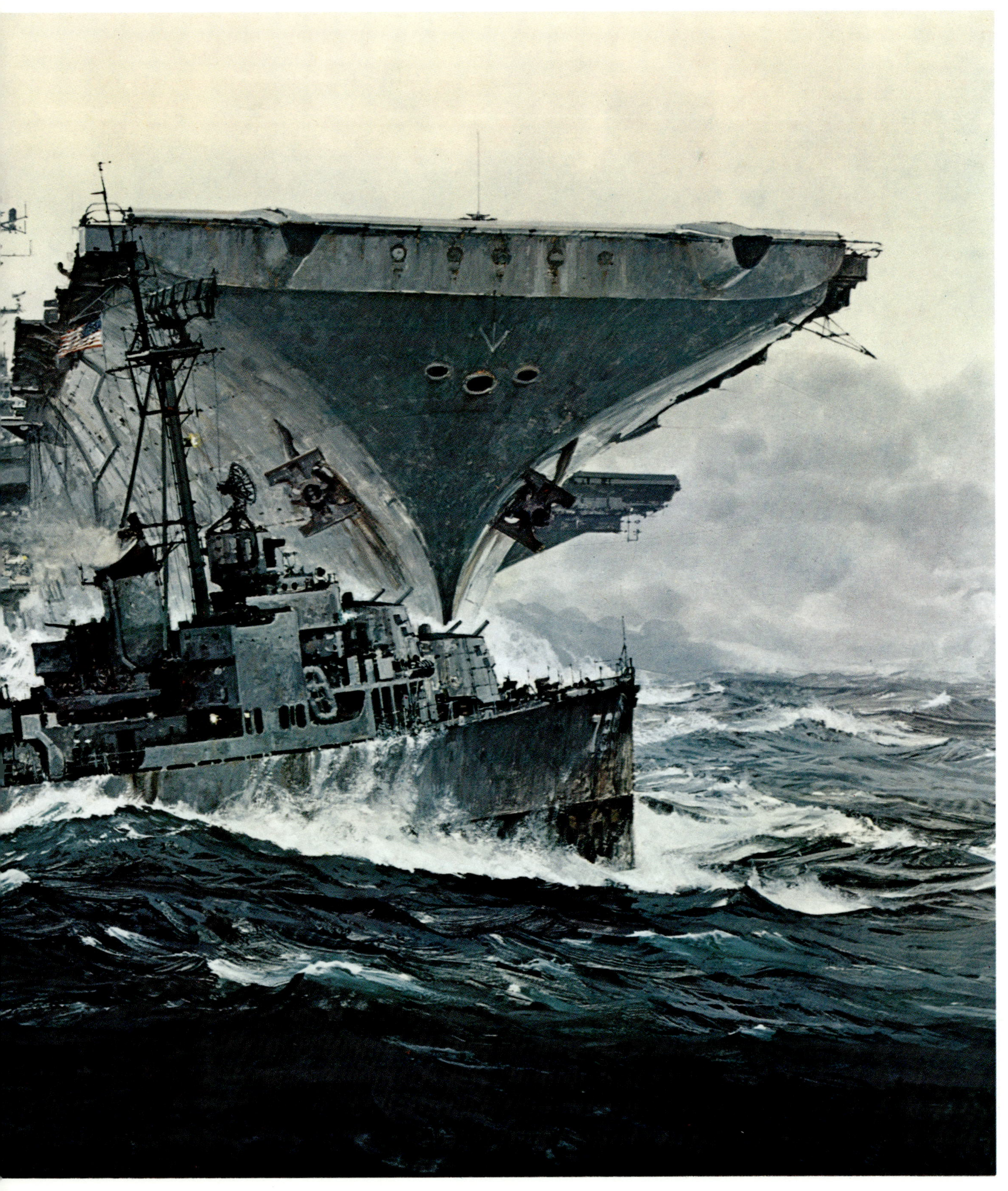

33) Ark Royal
by Kenneth Poolman
October 1973
New English Library

I like dramatic moments, this is when the
ship is sinking and the last of the crew were
being taken off.

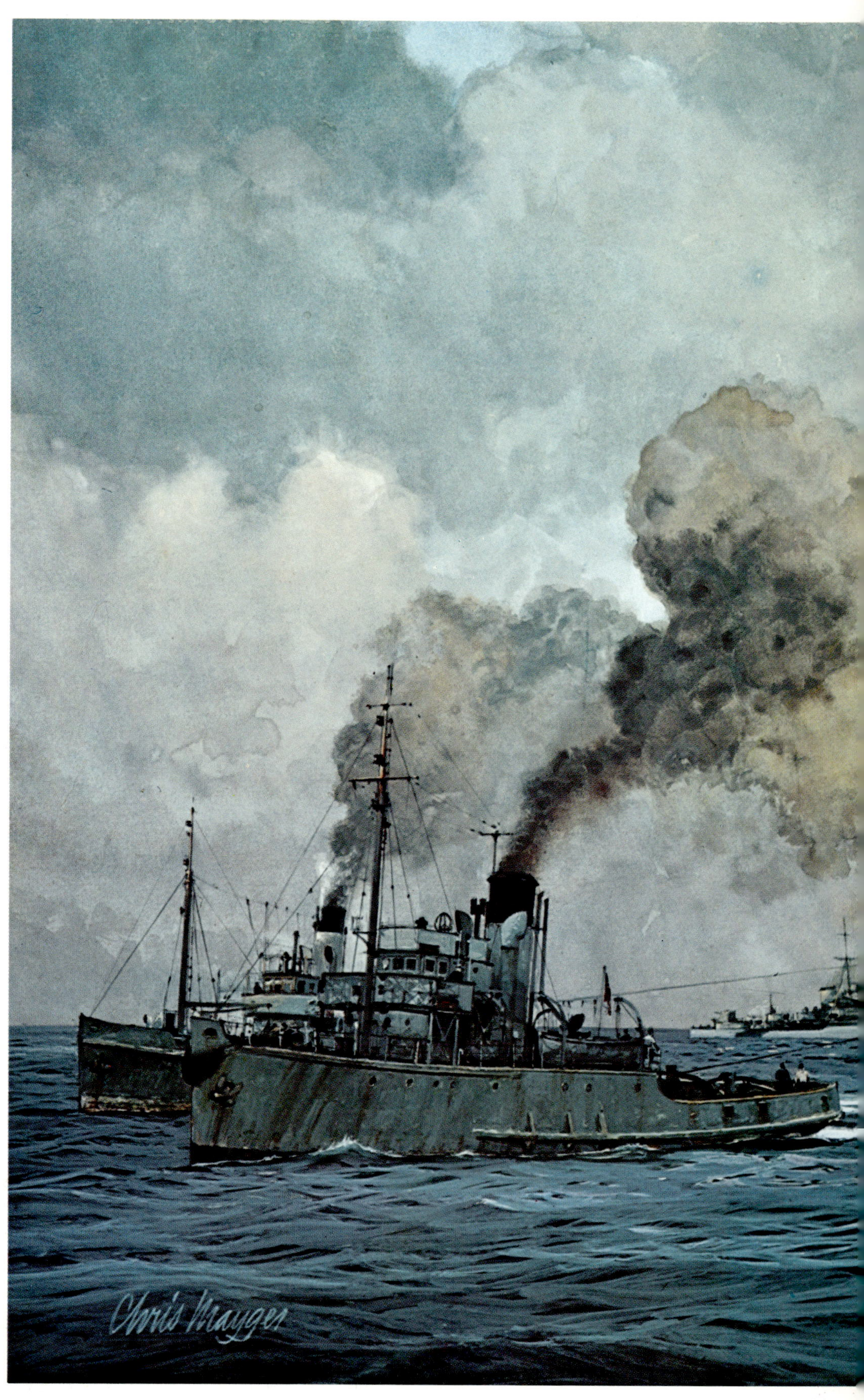

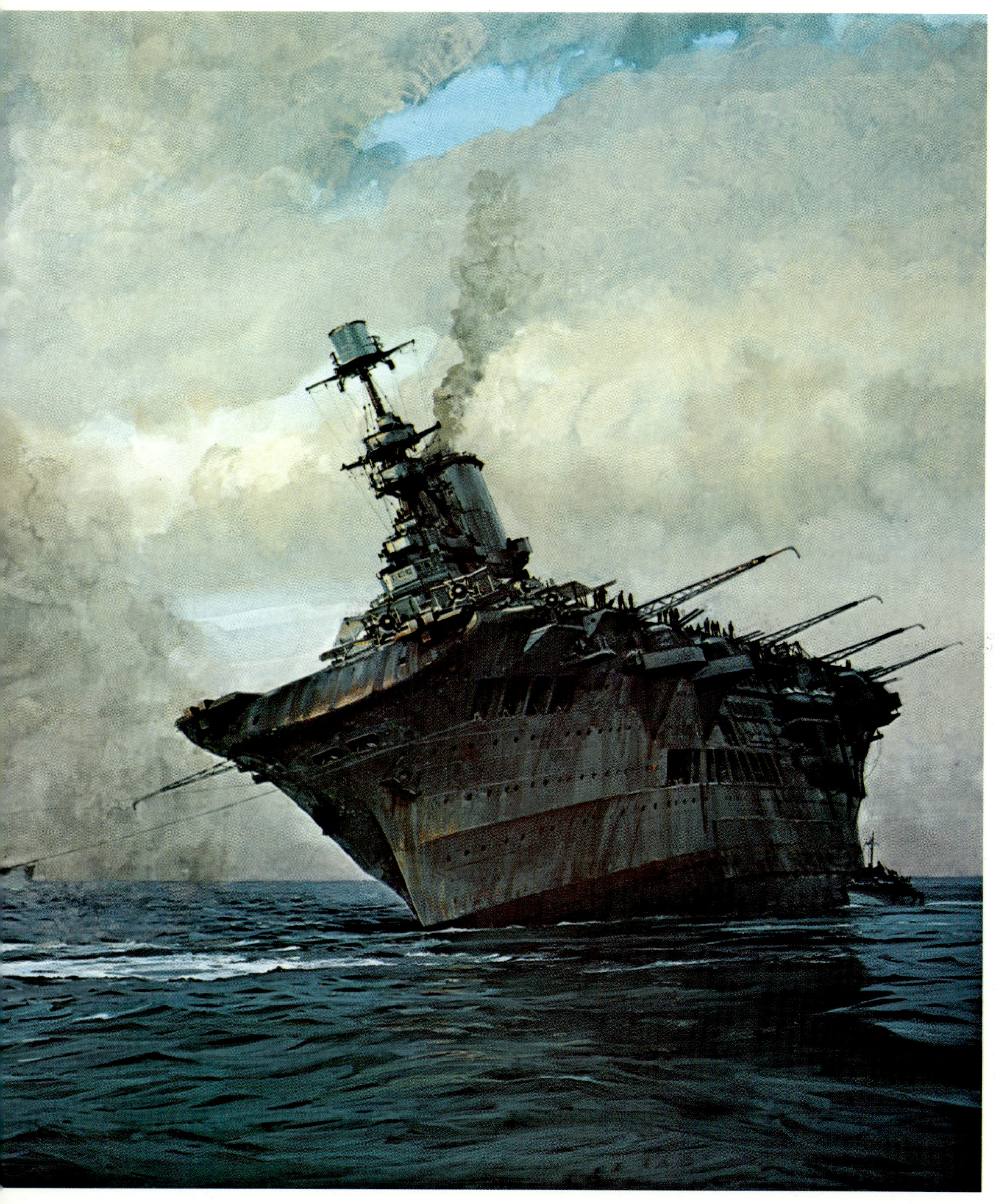

34) A Shackleton Called Sheila
by David Mariner
May 1971
New English Library

This story takes place in the near future and concerns one of the
last of the old-type prop planes used for air/sea rescue.

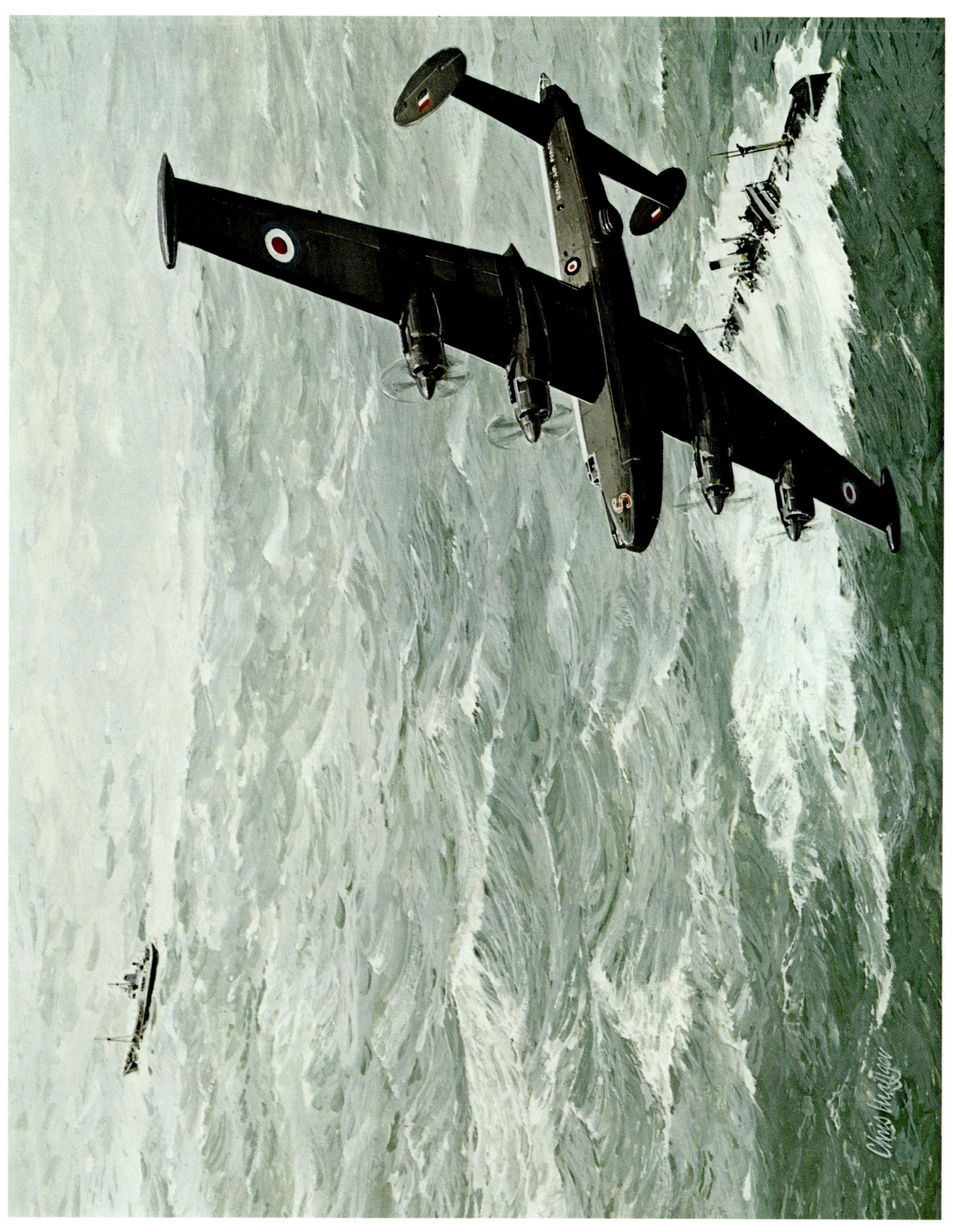

35) Trawlers go to War
by Paul Lund and Harry Ludlam
January 1972
New English Library

I had a visit from a man who once served on a trawler like this one. He said, 'it's the best picture he's seen.'

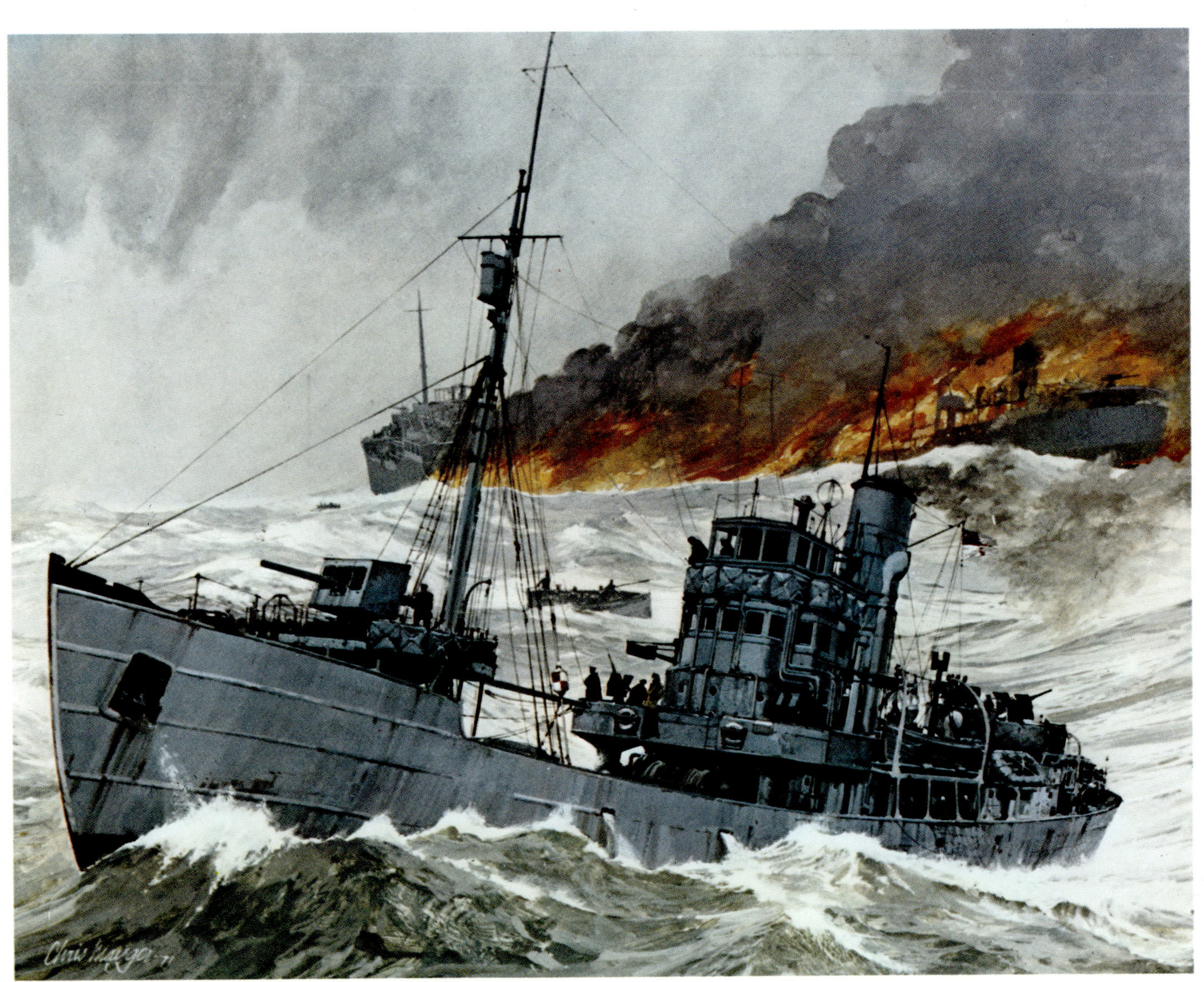

36) The K Boats
by Don Everitt
July 1971
New English Library
These were known as 'K' Class submarines, K for Kalamity!

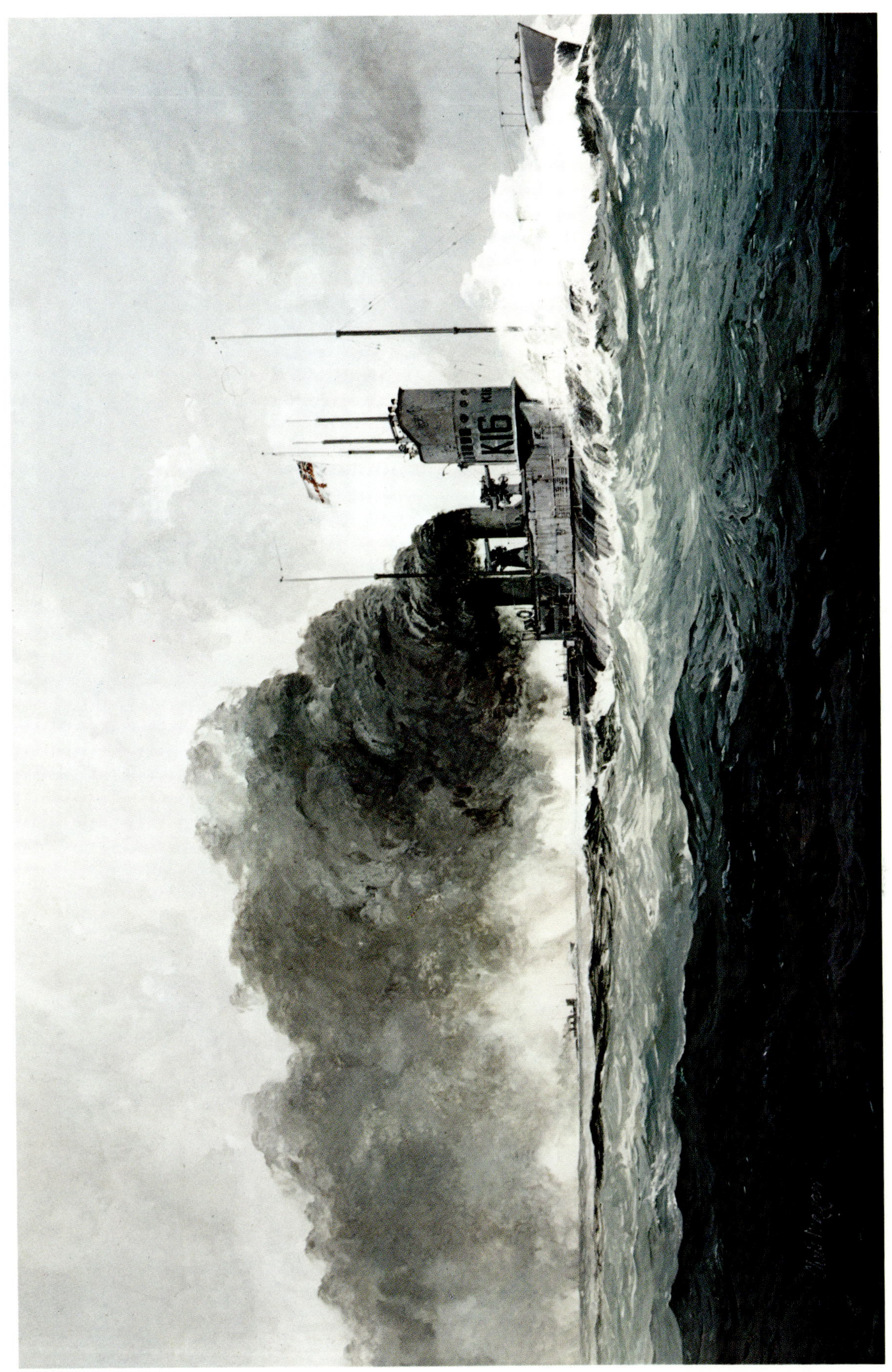

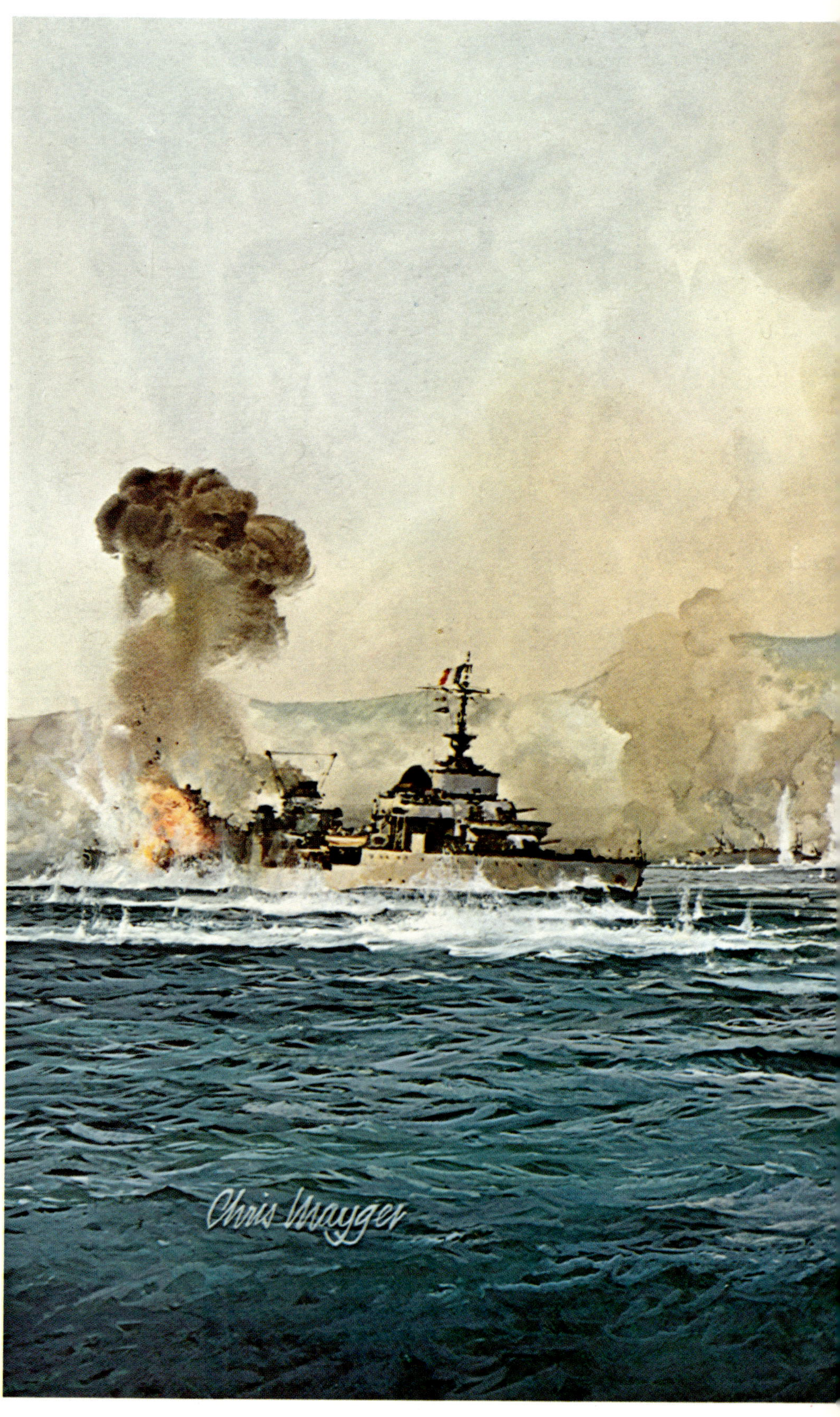

37) The Deadly Stroke
by Warren Tute
December 1975
Pan Books

This is the same incident as The Fleet
Without a Friend, *here I portrayed the
escape of the* Strasbourg, *a French
warship, as seen from the bows of a
French destroyer. I think my imagination
has improved.*

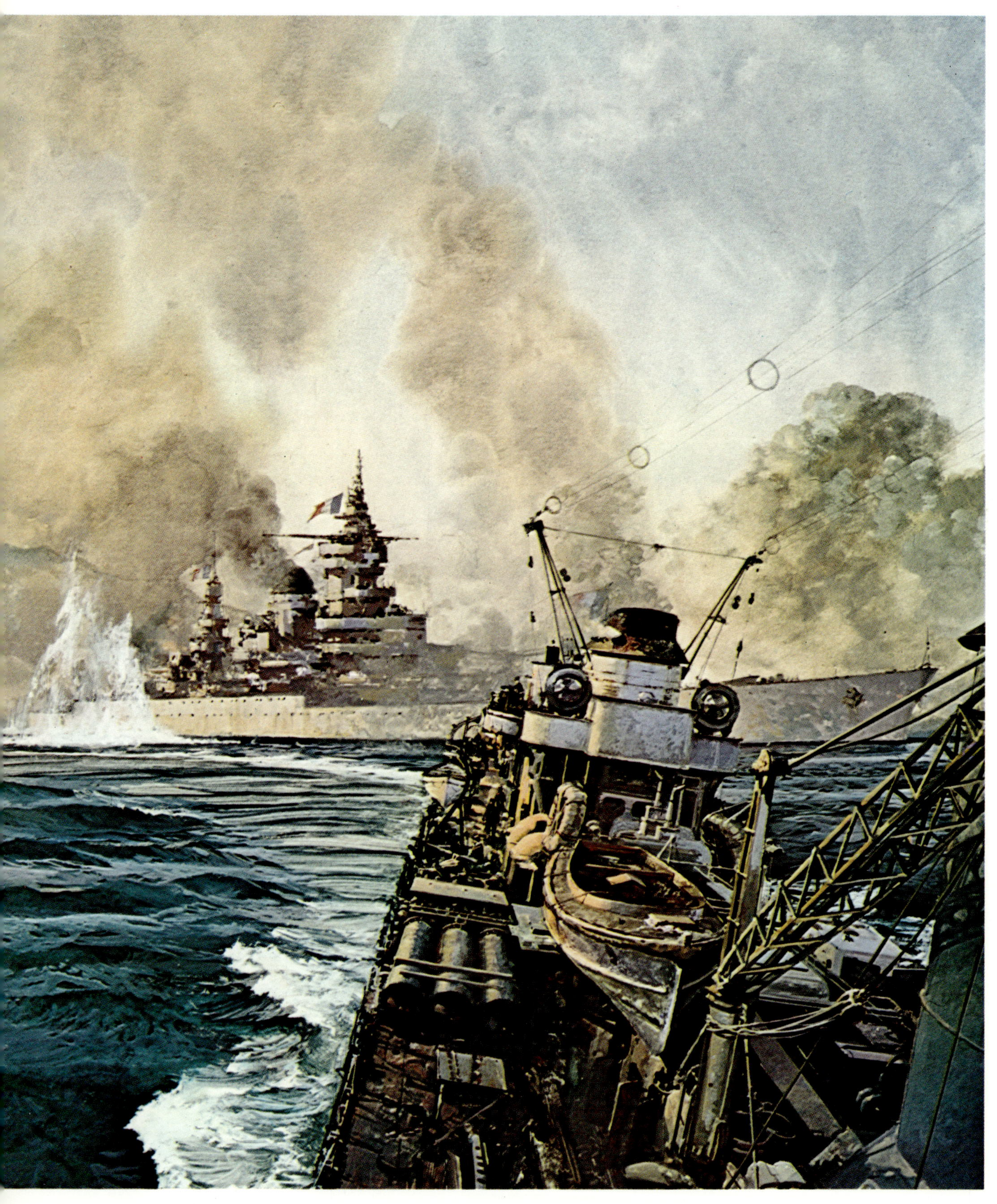

38) The Battle of the Torpedo Boats
by Bryan Cooper
March 1972
Pan Books

This painting is on loan to the Skipper of the 352. I wasn't as familiar with torpedo boats then as I am now. It is surprising comparing old work with new.

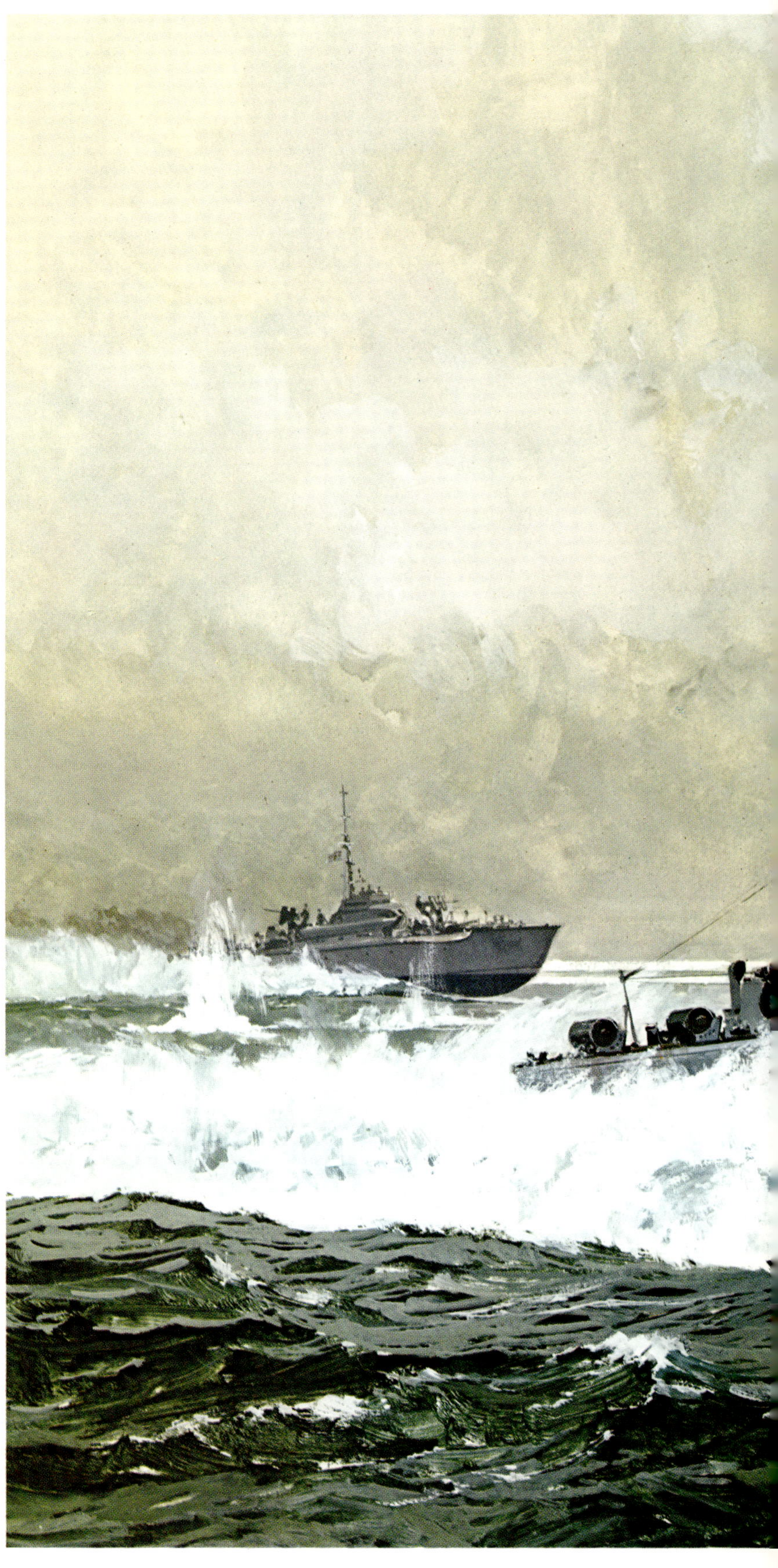

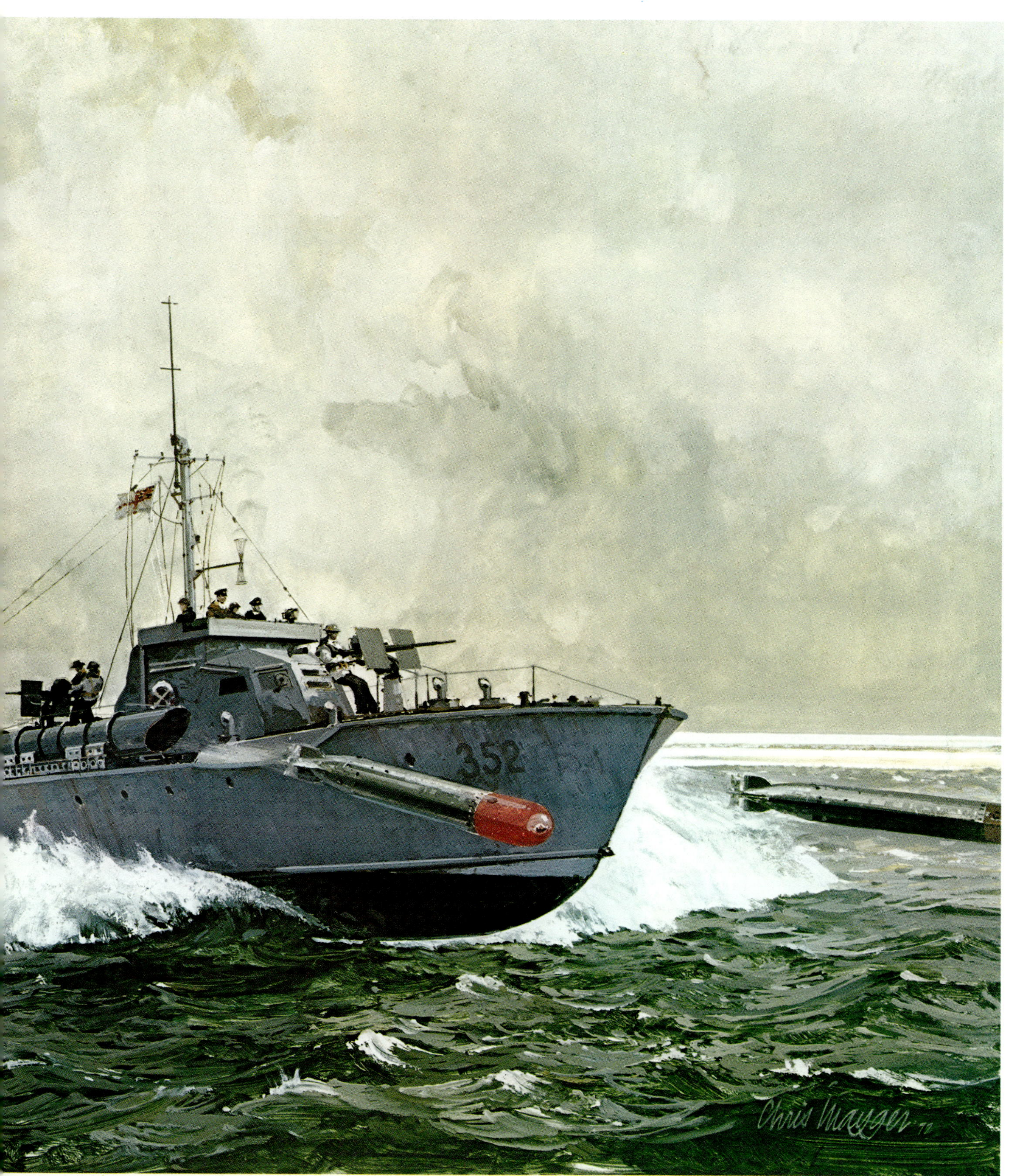

39) The German Navy in World
War Two
by Edward P. Von der Porten
February 1972
Pan Books

'Thunderbolt-Cereberus' – the Channel dash. This is the German Navy making their escape from Brest in 1942.

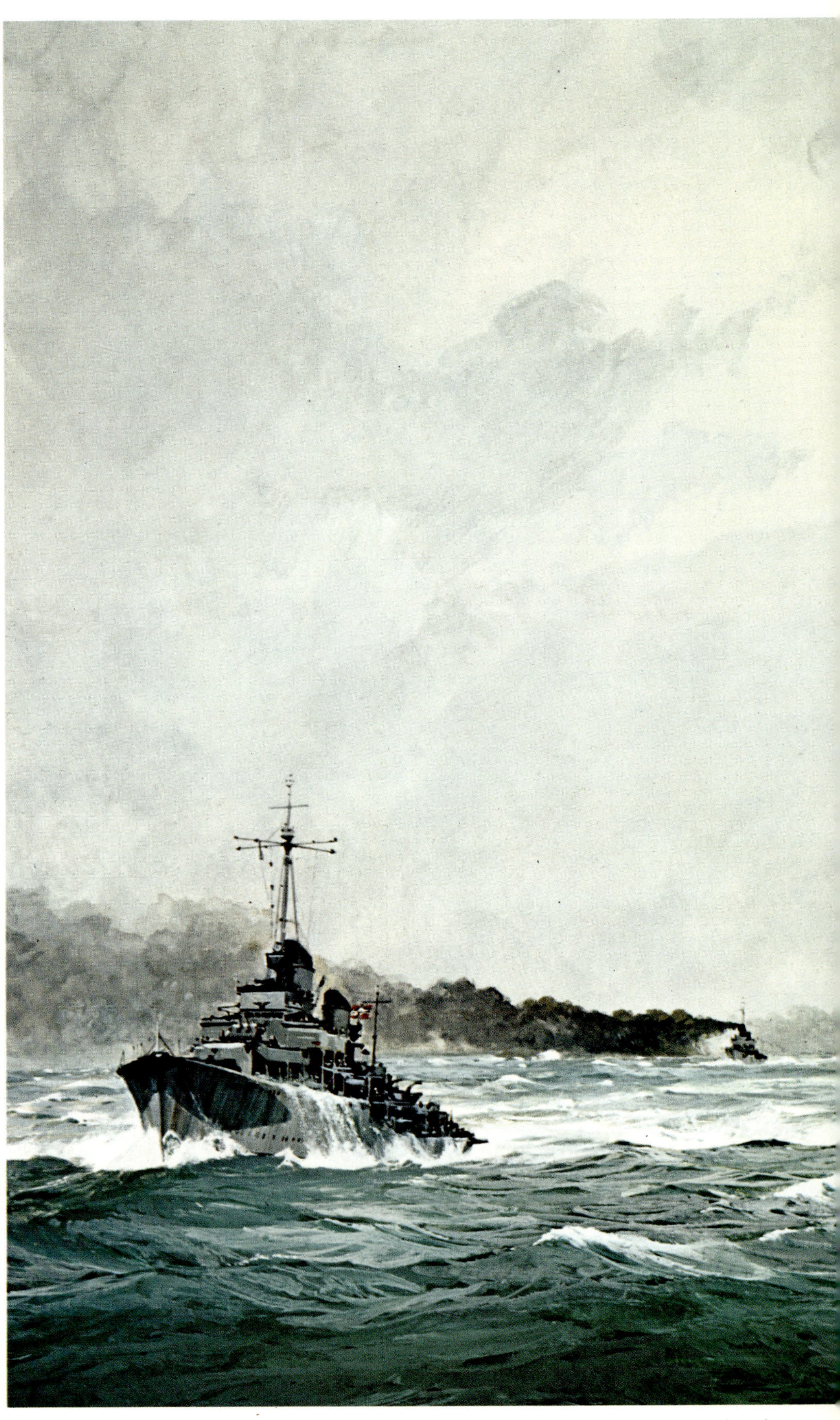

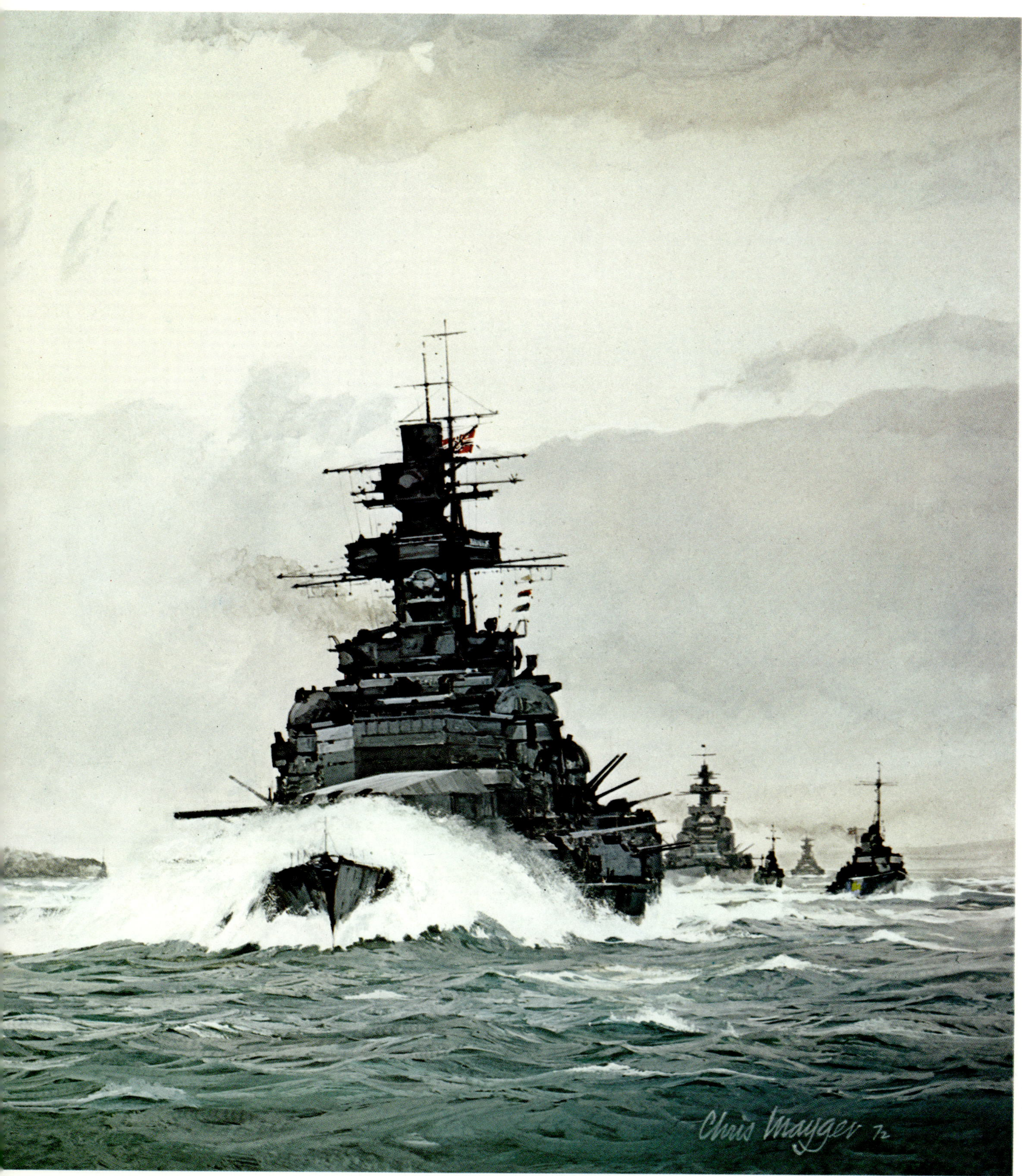

Chris Mayger 72

40) *Detail from*
The German Navy in World War Two
by Edward P. Von der Porten
February 1972
Pan Books

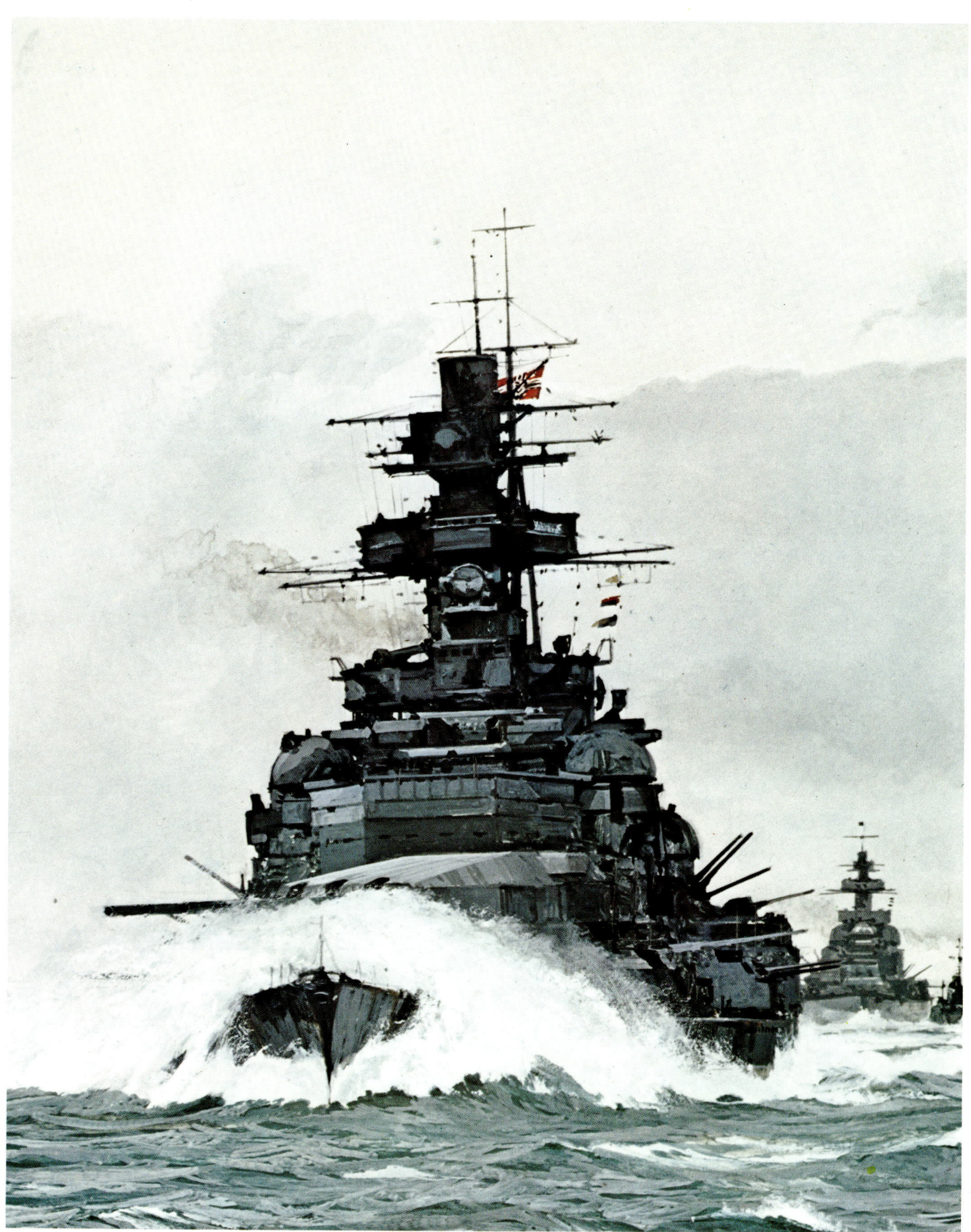